W9-AGZ-150

Ciro Cozzi
11/6/96

Ciro's Provincetown Kitchen

ITALIAN COOKING BY THE SEA

Recipes, tips and lore from the
acclaimed chef of Provincetown's
famous Italian restaurant,
Ciro & Sal's

Ciro Cozzi

with Alethea Cozzi

Illustrations by Ciro Cozzi

Mt. Ivy Press

© Copyright 1995 by
Ciro Cozzi and Alethea Cozzi

All rights reserved

Design: MC Design

Cover photos: David Henderson
of Eric Roth Photography

Printed in U.S.A.

ISBN 0-9635257-5-1

Mt. Ivy Press
P.O. Box 142
Boston, MA 02258
(617) 965-6306

Contents

INTRODUCTION

For four decades, visitors and locals alike have been streaming to the Provincetown restaurant known as CIRO & SAL'S. Many of these visitors are artists, both well-known and little known, and, from the beginning, they have played a major role, both as employees and as patrons, in the creation of this unique restaurant. They have lent to it a special atmosphere and have helped to spread its reputation for delicious—and abundant—Italian food, throughout the world.

The restaurant was established in the early 1950s by Ciro Cozzi and Sal Del Deo, who were both artists. The dishes on the menu are not restricted to any particular region of Italy: There are dishes from the south, from Rome, and from the north. However, all of the food has one thing in common—the creative touch of Ciro himself, who endlessly samples and experiments, while always insisting on high quality, excellent taste and ample portions. Here, at last, is the cookbook which will give you all the recipes for the dishes on CIRO & SAL'S menu, plus many more created by Ciro and his daughter Alethea.

In recent years, an interest in good food has developed all over the United States, and ingredients once difficult or even impossible to obtain can now be found in nearly every large supermarket, or, certainly, in specialty food stores. The ingredients needed to make the recipes in this book are not unusual: There are no secret substances, no expensive or rare spices—just the highest quality ingredients available for creating exciting and delicious food.

The cooking techniques used are just as straightforward as the ingredients. You need not order special equipment or take a cooking course. CIRO & SAL'S cooking secrets are revealed in an easy-to-follow format designed for the home cook. The finished dishes you serve will be the same as those enjoyed by the countless thousands who list a visit to CIRO & SAL'S, along with the sea and sun, as one of Provincetown's main attractions.

THE
RECIPES

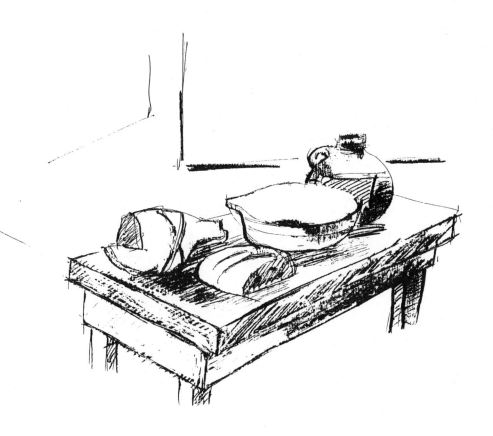

Antipasti
Appetizers

I first got to know Ciro in the spring of 1956. We were both working on the Air Force base in North Truro, Ciro as a carpenter and I as a laborer. Today, probably few people think of Ciro as a carpenter, but he was a fine craftsman (he had also worked at Flyer's Boatyard), and I acknowledge with gratitude the skills I learned from him.

In the restaurant's early years, Ciro had to do the carpentry work to supplement his income during the winter, when the restaurant was closed. Later, when he became more successful, Ciro designed and built additions onto the small, original cellar room, and construction usually went on until the last minute, as it did the time Ciro put the floor in in the back room the morning the restaurant opened. Ralph Santos, the great P-town mason, poured the floor and placed the flagstones in place, hoping that everything would set before the opening just a few hours away. Perhaps to divert the guests' attention away from their precarious footing, Ciro made the punch super-strong that night. Before long, everyone was floating euphorically over a floor that was still wet in places.

A year or two later Ciro, Eldred Mowery and I were putting up the main timbers of the upstairs dining room. The finale was the placement of the roof beam, a massive trunk that weighed over two hundred pounds. We manhandled the monster into place, secured it and went on to other things. Days later, we took down the scaffolding under the great beam and to our horror found that all that secured it was one six-penny nail.

For me, these episodes are the essence of Ciro—sometimes shaky underfoot, but always reaching for the sky, no matter what. Keep on, Ciro. Bravo!

TONY VEVERS

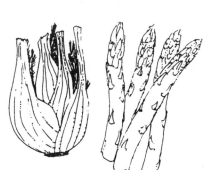

*A*ny of the salads and pasta salads can be used as appetizers or as part of an "antipasto composto." This would be a platter filled with a variety of foods. Here are some suggestions:

Sliced cured meats

Sliced cheeses

Cold, blanched vegetables dressed in extra virgin olive oil

Giardiniera (see recipe)

Suppli (see recipe)

Frittura composta (see recipe)

Frittata or frittata di pasta (see recipe), cut in wedges

Olives

Anchovies or sardines or tuna

Shellfish, poached and served dressed in olive oil and vinegar or herbed aioli.

Piatto misto (see recipe)

Aringa marinata (see recipe)

Ostriche al Giannini (see recipe)

Frittura Composta
Mixed Platter of Fried Foods

This is a platter of various meats, fish, vegetables and cheeses that have been cut into bite-size pieces, dipped in egg and flour, and fried in olive oil. The various foods are then arranged on a large platter and garnished with lemon wedges.

The frittura is usually served as a meal, but it may also be used as an appetizer or as part of an antipasto composto. How you compose the frittura is up to you. Try to get a variety of tastes and textures, although you can do a frittura composed entirely of fish or vegetables, if you so desire. Here are some possible ingredients:

Veal fillets (pounded and cut into thin strips)
Sweetbreads (cleaned and blanched*)
Brains (cleaned and blanched*)
Fish (if tiny, leave whole; if large, fillet and cut into thin strips)
Shrimp (whole)
Squid (cut into thick rings)
Artichoke hearts (cut in quarters)
Cauliflower flowerets (blanched)
Zucchini (cut into sticks)
Zucchini blossoms (whole with stamen removed)
Beets (sliced in thin circles)
Suppli (see recipe)
Mozzarella in Carozza (see recipe)

*To prepare the sweetbreads, soak them for ½ hour in cold water. Remove them from the water and place them in a casserole pan. Cover the sweetbreads with water and bring to a boil. Remove the pan from the heat and let the sweetbreads cool in their cooking water. Once cooled, remove them from the water, remove any excess membranes and cut them into 2-inch pieces. Pat dry.

*To prepare the brains, soak them as you would the sweetbreads. Place them in a casserole pan, cover them with cold water and add a pinch of salt and about a tablespoon of white vinegar. Bring the water to a boil, and just as soon as it boils, remove the brains and place in cold water to cool completely. Once cooled, remove them from the water and cut them into 1-inch pieces. Pat dry. The various foods can be prepared for frying in three ways.

First, they can be dipped in a pastella, or batter. To make the pastella, mix ½ cup flour with one cup water (it should be thick). Add a pinch of salt and 2 teaspoons olive oil. Just before you are ready to use the pastella, fold in 2 softly beaten egg whites. Dip in the pieces of food and fry. This works well with vegetables.

Second, simply dip the foods in flour seasoned with salt and pepper, and then dip them in beaten eggs also seasoned with salt and pepper. This works well with fishes and meats. If frying fish, try adding a little cornmeal to the flour.

Third, same as for the second method, but after dipping them in the egg, dip them in finely grated dry bread crumbs. This works well with cheeses and meats.

Fry the foods separately and try to keep the oil at the appropriate temperature. Medium heat works well with foods that have a high water content, like potatoes. Medium heat also works best for thick fish and meat. Higher heat is used for foods that are already partially or entirely cooked. Very high heat is used for small items that will cook quickly.

Drain the foods on paper towels or brown paper and keep in a warm (250 degree) oven until you have finished making the frittura.

Arrange all the foods on a platter. Garnish with sliced fresh lemon and chopped parsley. Serve immediately.

Giardiniera
Marinated Vegetables

1.   Cut an assortment of vegetables in bite-size cubes, circles and flowerets. The giardiniera should be colorful, so choose your vegetables accordingly (cauliflower, carrots, broccoli, beets, celery, sweet red peppers, zucchini, etc.). Blanche and shock the vegetables separately. (See Glossary for cooking technique.) Pat them dry.

2.   Layer the vegetables in a glass jar and cover them with white wine vinegar. Seal the jar and let the vegetables marinate for at least 24 hours. The giardiniera can be served as is, or it can be tossed with extra virgin olive oil, Maionese or Aioli, and seasoned further with fresh herbs, salt and pepper. Serve as part of an antipasto.

Cuori Di Carciofi Sott' Olio
Artichoke Hearts in Olive Oil
Serves 4

12	fresh artichokes	1	teaspoon dried basil or chopped fresh basil leaves
	Juice of 1 lemon		Salt and freshly ground
	Salt		black pepper
¼	cup extra virgin olive oil	4	lemon wedges or slices
1	tablespoon fresh lemon juice		
1	garlic clove, pressed		

1.   Remove all the leaves and the chokes from the artichokes. Cook the artichoke hearts in simmering water, with the lemon juice and salt to taste until they are tender. They should still be firm (al dente). Drain and cool.

2.   In a bowl, mix together all the remaining ingredients except the lemon wedges. Add the artichoke hearts and toss to mix thoroughly. Marinate at room temperature for 3 hours before serving with the lemon wedges.

Asparagi con Prosciutto
Asparagus with Prosciutto
Serves 4

24   thin asparagus spears

8   thin slices prosciutto, trimmed of excess fat

1.   Break or cut off the tough parts of the asparagus stems so that all of the spears are of equal length. Steam the asparagus until they are tender but firm (al dente). Plunge the cooked spears into ice water to stop the cooking, then drain and dry thoroughly.

2.   Gather 3 spears together in a bundle and wrap a slice of prosciutto around the spears. Make 7 additional bundles in the same way.

3.   Lightly dress each bundle with extra virgin olive oil or Pesto (page 119) to which extra olive oil has been added.

Ripiene di Zucchini
Zucchini Stuffed with Crabmeat
Serves 4 to 6

1½	pounds small zucchini
¼	cup fresh bread crumbs, no crust
1½	tablespoons chopped parsley
½	cup Parmigiano, grated
8	ounces crabmeat, drained and tossed with a few drops olive oil

	Black pepper
8	leaves of fresh basil, chopped
⅓	cup olive oil
1	pound fresh tomatoes
	Salt to taste

1.   Drop tomatoes in boiling water for 2 minutes. Peel off skins and squeeze out seeds. Chop pulp into small pieces.

2.   Gently scrub zucchini. Trim ends. Cut zucchini in half lengthwise. Scoop out pulp and finely chop it.

3.   Soak the crumbs in a little white wine or water, then squeeze tightly to remove liquid. In a bowl combine the bread crumbs, crabmeat, parsley, cheese, basil, ground pepper and chopped zucchini pulp. Mix well. Stuff the mix into the zucchini shells.

4.   Place zucchini in a skillet with heated olive oil. Brown lightly. Remove to a platter.

5.   Add tomatoes to skillet and cook for 10 minutes at moderate heat. Return zucchini to pan, add salt and cook at low heat for another 5 to 6 minutes. Serve with a parsley garnish.

Caponata
Marinated Eggplant
Serves 8

2	medium-size eggplants, cut into ¾-inch cubes	¾	cup capers, rinsed and drained
	Salt	½	cup pitted green olives, cut in half
¾	cup olive oil		
1	cup celery cut into large dice	3	tablespoons red wine vinegar
2	medium-size onions, cut into large dice	1	teaspoon sugar
			Salt and freshly ground black pepper
1	28-ounce can imported Italian plum tomatoes, drained, seeded and chopped		

1.   Put the eggplant cubes into a colander and sprinkle them with salt. Weight them down with a plate and let drain for 30 minutes. Rinse the eggplant in cool running water and dry it well.
2.   Heat the oil in a saucepan and cook the eggplant until it is lightly browned. Remove the eggplant with a slotted spoon, leaving the oil in the pan.
3.   Add the onions and celery to the pan and cook until the onions are translucent. Add the tomatoes and cook for 12 minutes.
4.   Add the eggplant, capers, olives, vinegar, sugar and salt and pepper to taste. Cook over low heat for 8 minutes. Serve hot or at room temperature.

Funghi Sott' Olio e Aceto
Marinated Mushrooms
Serves 4 to 6

1	pound fresh mushrooms	¼	cup fresh lemon juice
2	garlic cloves, pressed	2	tablespoons red wine vinegar
¼	teaspoon ground turmeric		Salt and freshly ground
½	cup extra virgin olive oil		pepper

1.   Cut the ends from the stems of the mushrooms. Wash or wipe the mushrooms thoroughly; then cut them into thick slices.

2.   Mix together all the remaining ingredients in a bowl and add the mushrooms. Toss to mix well, being careful not to break the mushrooms. Marinate at room temperature for at least 3 hours before serving.

Mozzarella in Carozza
Mozzarella in a Carriage
Serves 4

4	large eggs, beaten	1	cup fine bread crumbs,
½	cup heavy cream		toasted
	Salt and freshly ground	2	cups vegetable oil
	black pepper		
12	¾-inch-thick slices fresh		
	mozzarella		

1.   Mix together the eggs and cream. Season with salt and pepper. Dip the slices of mozzarella into the egg wash and let the excess drip off.
2.   Season the bread crumbs with salt and pepper. Pat the mozzarella slices into the crumbs to coat them thoroughly.
3.   Heat the oil to 350 degrees in a heavy skillet. Fry the mozzarella for 1 minute on each side, or until golden brown. Drain briefly on paper tow-

Mozzarella in Carozza con Acciughe
Mozzarella in a Carriage with Anchovies
Serves 2 to 4

8	¼-inch-thick slices Italian bread	¼	cup all-purpose flour
4	¼-inch-thick slices fresh mozzarella	2	large eggs
4	anchovy fillets, rinsed, dried and coarsely chopped		Pinch of salt
		¼	cup olive oil

1.   Remove the crusts from the bread and cut each slice in half on the diagonal to create two triangles. Ideally, the triangles should be about 2 inches long and 1 inch wide at the base.

2.   Cut the slices of mozzarella to fit the bread triangles. Place each slice of mozzarella on a slice of bread. Add a little of the chopped anchovies. Cover with another slice of bread to create a sandwich.

3.   Dip only the edges of the sandwiches in the flour. This will keep the mozzarella from oozing out when it is cooked.

4.   Now place a small amount of tepid water in a low, flat pan and moisten the floured edges of the sandwich in the water. Set the sandwiches on a plate. They should not touch.

5.   Beat the eggs and salt in a shallow pan large enough to hold all the sandwiches. Arrange all the sandwiches in the pan and allow them to absorb the eggs for 15 to 20 minutes on each side. All the egg should be absorbed.

6.   Heat the oil in a skillet and fry the sandwiches until they are golden brown on both sides. Drain briefly on paper towels and serve immediately.

Pomodori Fargiti
Ripe Tomatoes Stuffed with Eggs, Anchovies, Capers and Basil
Serves 6 to 8

3	large hard-boiled eggs	8	ripe tomatoes
12	anchovy fillets	2	scallions, finely chopped
5	tablespoons capers, washed and drained	2	tablespoons minced fresh basil

1.   In a processor combine the eggs, anchovies and 4 tablespoons of capers. Blend until creamy.

2.   Cut the tomatoes in half, from stem down. Remove the pulp, leave a good amount around the sides. Mix the scallions and basil with the blended eggs.

3.   Stuff the tomatoes and sprinkle the tops with a few capers. Serve at room temperature, garnished with fresh basil.

Cannellini Toscano
Tuscan Style Beans
Serves 6

1	pound small navy beans, washed	4	garlic cloves, peeled and trimmed
1	cup virgin olive oil	2	teaspoons salt and a few flakes of red pepper
2	bay leaves	1	tablespoon white wine vinegar
4	fresh sage leaves		

1.   Place beans in a stock pot with 8 cups of water, 3 tablespoons of oil, bay leaves, sage leaves, garlic and salt. Bring to a boil, reduce heat and simmer until beans are soft. Beans will absorb most of water.

2.   Remove sage and bay leaves and let beans cool.

3.   Purée beans in a processor, add remaining olive oil and blend to a smooth consistency. Garnish with fresh sage. Serve as a dip with crusty bread.

Bruschette
Toasted Bread with Olive Oil

These are perfect for a light meal or as hors d'oeuvres.

The basic technique is very simple. Take a thick slice of Italian bread, rub both sides of the bread with a slice of garlic. (This can also be done after the bread has been toasted.) Sprinkle a generous amount of extra virgin olive oil on both sides. Toast the bread in the oven, broil it or grill it on both sides until it is crispy on the outside but still soft on the inside. Be careful not to burn it.

The bruschette may be eaten as is or with a variety of toppings. Here are some suggestions:

Fresh mozzarella, tomatoes and basil
Tomato slices and salt
A purée of cannellini beans and tuna
Fagioli al Fiasco (see recipe)
Sliced Italian cured meats (especially prosciutto)

Fazzoletti Ripieno
Stuffed "Handkerchiefs"
Serves 12

12	10-inch crepes (page 107)	1	pound boiled ham or
4	medium zucchini, diced		cappacola, diced
4	fresh tomatoes, peeled and	½	pound fontina cheese, diced
	chopped	1	cup grated Parmigiano
		4	egg whites

1.   Combine vegetables, ham and cheeses.
2.   Place 2 tablespoons mixture on half of crepe. Brush edges with egg white. Fold over and seal. Lay on a well-buttered sheet. Make soft folds so crepes resemble a handkerchief.
3.   Brush tops with egg white and sprinkle with remaining Parmigiano. Cover with buttered foil and bake 10 minutes in a 350-degree oven.

NOTE: Use your creativity in arranging the folds of the crepes. These "handkerchiefs" make a very pretty first course.

Fazzoletti con Funghi Secci e Prosciutto

Handkerchiefs (Crepes) with Porcini Mushrooms and Prosciutto

Serves 12

This is reminiscent of a big, delicate ravioli.

12	10-inch crepes (page 107)	2	cups bread fresh crumbs
1	cup dried porcini mushrooms	½	cup grated Parmigiano
½	cup (1 stick) butter, melted	2	cups Balsamella sauce
2	large onions, finely chopped		(page 267)
1	pound boiled ham, cut into strips		Salt and pepper

1.   Soak mushrooms in warm water to cover for 15 minutes. Chop coarsely.

2.   Sauté onions in 4 tablespoons melted butter until wilted. Add ham and soaked mushrooms with their water. Simmer 5 minutes.

3.   Add ½ cup Balsamella. Brush each crepe with butter, sprinkle with a spoonful of bread crumbs, place a spoonful of mushroom mixture on half the crepe and fold other half over top.

4.   Place crepes on a buttered oven pan, not touching, cover with buttered foil and bake for 12 minutes at 350 degrees. Combine grated Parmigiano with remaining Balsamella and heat. Serve as a sauce.

Supplì
Filled Rice Balls
Serves 6

12	ounces (about 2 cups) Arborio rice		2	tablespoons butter
1	cup Sugo di Pomodoro Semplice (page 115)		2	ounces grated Parmigiano
1½	cups water		2	large eggs, beaten

FILLINGS

Mozzarella, cut into small cubes
Chopped prosciutto
Sautéed chopped onions
Chopped fresh herbs
Sautéed chopped fresh mushrooms

Pre-soaked chopped porcini mushrooms
Pecorino or caciotta, chopped
1   cup fine dry breadcrumbs
2   cups olive oil or vegetable oil

1.   Put the rice, tomato sauce and water in a saucepan. Cover the pan and bring to a boil. Lower the heat and simmer the rice until it is tender. There should be no excess liquid.
2.   Remove the pan from the heat and stir in the butter, grated cheese and eggs. Fresh herbs may be added at this point. Turn the mixture out onto a plate. Spread it over the plate and let it cool completely.
3.   Prepare the filling of your choice.
4.   Put a rounded tablespoon of rice into the palm of your hand. Make a well in the center and add a little bit of the filling. Squeeze the rice over and around the filling to form a compact ball. Roll the ball in the bread crumbs, covering it entirely. Put the completed rice ball on a baking sheet. Continue making rice balls in this way until all the rice has been used. Be sure that the rice balls do not touch on the baking sheet.

5.   Heat the oil in a large pan with low sides, being careful not to let the oil get so hot that it smokes. Fry the rice balls in the oil until they are golden all over. Drain them on brown paper or paper towels and serve immediately.

6.   The Suppli can be served as an hors d'oeuvre, an appetizer, a snack or as part of a frittura composta.

Prosciutto con Melone
Prosciutto with Melon
Serves 4

1	ripe cantaloupe or honeydew melon	4	lemon wedges or slices
½	pound prosciutto, thinly sliced and trimmed of excess fat		

1.   Cut the melon in half from top to bottom. Remove the seeds and membranes. Then cut the melon into 1-inch-thick slices and remove the rind.

2.   Arrange the wedges on a serving plate. Lay the slices of prosciutto across the wedges of fruit, or wrap the prosciutto around the wedges. Serve with lemon wedges.

Carpaccio di Bue
Raw Beef Tenderloin with Olive Oil and Parmigiano
Serve 6 to 8

2	pounds tenderloin of beef, close trim	½	cup virgin olive oil fresh herbs for garnish
2	tablespoons capers	1	lemon, wedged
1	cup Parmigiano shavings		

1.   Trim tenderloin of all fat. For a less expensive cut, use eye of the round. Slice beef very thin, no more than ⅟₁₆-inch thick. Arrange on a serving platter.

2.   Spread capers over slices. Make Parmigiano shavings with a vegetable peeler and sprinkle on top. Drizzle oil on entire surface. Garnish platter with lemon wedges and fresh herbs (basil, chervil, parsley, etc.)

Carpaccio con Capperi
Raw Beef with Capers
Serves 6

1	pound raw, lean, beef fillet	6	anchovy fillets, rinsed and drained
½	cup extra virgin olive oil		
¼	cup fresh lemon juice	1	teaspoon Dijon mustard
¼	cup plus 2 tablespoons capers, rinsed and drained	2	garlic cloves, finely chopped
		¼	teaspoon freshly ground black pepper

1.   Trim the beef of all the outside fat.

2.   Slice the meat very thinly. An electric slicer works best for this. It is essential that the meat be sliced as thinly as possible.

3.   Put the oil, lemon juice, ¼ cup of the capers, anchovy fillets, Dijon mustard, garlic and black pepper in a food processor or blender and process until smooth.

4.   Arrange the slices of meat, overlapping, on a flat serving plate. The plate should be completely covered. Garnish the meat with the remaining 2 tablespoons of capers. Serve the sauce on the side.

Crostini
Grilled Bread with Paté

½	pound liver pate	½	cup olive oil
8	slices of a good French or Italian bread, ½-inch thick, cut in rounds, squares or triangles		Salt and pepper to taste Water cress and olives to garnish
2	cloves minced garlic		

1.   Let paté stand at room temperature until soft. Brush bread with olive oil, minced garlic, salt and pepper. Grill lightly until brown.

2.   Spread paté about ¼- to ½-inch thick on hot bread. Garnish with black and green olives and sprigs of watercress. Serve 2 or 3 crostini per person.

Paté di Campagna
Country Paté
Serves 8 to 10

2	pounds fatty pork, ground	2	tablespoons salt
2	pounds fatty veal, ground	1½	teaspoons freshly ground
1	pound pork livers or calf's liver, ground		white pepper
		¾	cup cognac
1	cup cooked ham or tongue, diced	1½	pounds fresh pork fat, thinly sliced
1½	cups finely chopped onion	5	bay leaves
6	garlic cloves, finely chopped	1	tablespoon chopped fresh
1	teaspoon dried thyme		rosemary leaves
1	teaspoon ground allspice		

1.   Combine all the ingredients, except the pork fat, bay leaves and rosemary, in a ceramic or enamel bowl. Mix thoroughly, cover, and refrigerate overnight.

2.   The next day preheat the oven to 350 degrees. Line the bottom and sides of a 5- by 9- by 3-inch loaf pan with the pork fat. Allow the fat to hang over the sides by about 2 inches. Press the meat mixture firmly into the loaf pan. Bang the pan on the table a couple of times to make sure the meat is firmly settled in the pan. Fold the pork fat over the meat to cover it. Lay the bay leaves in a single row down the center and sprinkle the rosemary over the entire surface.

3.   Cover the pan tightly with a double thickness of aluminum foil. Place the paté pan into a slightly larger pan and fill this pan with enough warm water to reach halfway up the sides of the paté pan. Bake the paté for 1½ hours.

4.   When the paté has finished cooking, remove it from the pan with the water and let it cool at room temperature for 1 hour. Next, place a pan that

is slightly smaller than the paté mold on top of the paté. Fill the pan with heavy objects. Refrigerate the weighted-down paté overnight.

5.   The next day remove the weights and the foil from the pate. Dip the pan in hot water and turn the paté out onto a plate. Serve immediately or cover tightly and keep refrigerated until you are ready to use it. (The paté will keep for a week.)

Cozze alla San Marco
Mussels in the Style of San Marco
Serves 2

½	cup olive oil	3	tablespoon chervil, finely chopped
½	bunch fennel tops, finely chopped	¼	teaspoon red pepper flakes
10	scallions, finely chopped	60	mussels
12	anchovies, minced	30	green olives, finely chopped
10	tomatoes, peeled, seeded, finely chopped	½	cup dry sherry
		½	cup dry vermouth

1.   In a large skillet heat olive oil and sauté scallions and fennel. When soft, add anchovies. Cook a few minutes then add tomatoes, herbs, olives, and sherry. Remove from heat after ten minutes.

2.   While sauce is cooking steam mussels with a little oil and the vermouth. When mussels have opened, remove from pot and put them on a platter. Then spoon sauce over mussels. Serve hot or cold.

Vongole Marinate
Marinated Clams
Serves 8

¼   cup olive oil
48   little neck clams
1   large red onion
2   cloves garlic, minced
4   slices prosciutto or pancetta, chopped
½   cup celery hearts, chopped fine

2   fresh tomatoes, peeled and seeded
¼   teaspoon fresh minced rosemary
12   fresh basil leaves
½   cup red wine

1.   Heat oil in a large saucepan, add chopped onion and garlic. When garlic turns color, add prosciutto. Cook at low heat for 5 minutes, then add celery, tomatoes and herbs.

2.   Continue cooking for 10 minutes, then add wine, cover and cook until clams have opened.

4.   Cool. Remove clams from shell. Refrigerate for 24 hours. Shells may be used for garnish. This also is excellent served hot, with a thin pasta - cappelini, spaghettini, etc.

Cozze Marinate
Marinated Mussels
Serves 8

60-80 mussels, bearded and washed
¼ cup olive oil
2 cups white wine
¼ cup white wine vinegar
¼ cup Dijon mustard
1 cup scallions, chopped coarse
4 cloves garlic, chopped fine

1 teaspoon oregano
1 teaspoon rosemary
½ cup parsley, finely chopped
1 lemon, juice of
2 lemon slices
Pepper, black and red, to taste

1. Heat the oil in a large saucepan, add garlic and sauté until it is golden.
2. Add the remaining ingredients, cover and simmer until mussels have opened, about 10 minutes. Place in a ceramic bowl and refrigerate until chilled.
3. Garnish with lemon slices and parsley.

Spiedini di Capesante
Skewered Scallops
Serves 2

4	pearl onions, peeled	6	artichoke hearts, marinated in oil
4	sea scallops		
4	large mushroom caps	¼	cup olive oil
1	red bell pepper, sliced lengthwise		pepper and salt
		3	large garlic cloves, chopped
1	green bell pepper, sliced lengthwise		Fresh rosemary and lemon slices for garnish

1.   Toss together all the ingredients except garnish. Let stand, refrigerated, for 1 hour.

2.   Prepare skewers. Alternate ingredients: Scallop, artichoke, mushroom cap, red pepper, green pepper and onion. Repeat until skewer is filled. Cook under broiler, turning often, or grill over charcoal.

3.   Remove from skewer and arrange nicely on heated plates, sprinkle with olive oil, garnish with lemon and fresh rosemary.

Capesante con Balsamico
Scallops with Balsamic Vinegar
Serves 4, hot or cold

MARINADE

½   cup olive oil
⅓   cup balsamic vinegar
¼   cup fresh mint
¼   cup fresh thyme or ½
     teaspoon dry

⅛   cup fresh parsley, minced
4   cloves garlic, minced.
     Juice of 1 lemon

1   pound raw scallops, bay or sea
2   slices prosciutto, fat trimmed,
     minced

Mint and lemon slices for
garnish

1.   Combine marinade ingredients and cook over medium heat for 15 minutes. Turn off heat.
2.   When cool, add scallops and prosciutto. Refrigerate for 24 hours. Can be served hot or cold. If serving hot, heat at low heat for a few minutes. Garnish with fresh mint and lemon slices.

NOTE: As in the Spanish dish called Seviche, the scallops "cook" in the acidic marinade.

Piatto Misto
Marinated Shellfish
Serves 4 to 6

½	pound unshelled medium-size shrimp	½	cup extra virgin olive oil
½	pound sea scallops	¼	cup fresh lemon juice
1½	dozen mussels, scrubbed and debearded	2	garlic cloves, pressed
4	tablespoons red wine vinegar	¼	teaspoon dried marjoram
			Salt and freshly ground black pepper

1.   Bring 3 quarts of water to a boil and add a tablespoon of the vinegar. Add the shrimp and scallops and return the water to a boil. Cook the shellfish for 2 minutes, then drain and rinse in cold water.

2.   Put the mussels in a saucepan with ¼ inch of water. Cover the pan and cook over medium heat until the shells open. Remove them from the pan and let cool. Remove the mussels from the shells.

3.   Shell and devein the shrimp.

4.   Combine the shellfish in a bowl. Blend together the remaining ingredients and pour the dressing over the shellfish. Toss well to mix. Cover and refrigerate for 2 hours before serving.

Insalate di Mare
Seafood Salad
Serves 6 to 8

16	shrimp, peeled and deveined	8	squid
1	pound scallops, bay or sea	16	oysters
16	mussels	3	Belgian endive

MARINADE

¼	cup white wine vinegar	¼	cup lemon juice
¼	cup olive oil	¼	teaspoon red pepper flakes
12	anchovies, minced		
2	tablespoons fresh rosemary or fresh basil, minced		

1.   Peel and devein shrimp; leave tails. Bay scallops leave whole. Cut sea scallops in quarters. Clean mussels. Clean squid, peel skin and remove beak but save the tentacles. Open oysters. Slice endive ¼-inch thick across grain.
2.   Combine marinade ingredients in a large pan. Bring to a boil, then reduce to simmer.
2.   Add shrimp and mussels. When mussels begin to open, add scallops. Cook for 2 minutes covered over low heat, then turn off heat and add squid and oysters.
3.   When mixture has cooled add endive. Serve chilled. It is better to allow 24 hours before serving. Serve on a bed of whole endive leaves. Garnish with fresh rosemary.

Insalata di Aragosta
Lobster Salad
Serves 2

1   2-pound lobster, cooked and
     shelled. Save body shell. Cut
     tail into ½-inch slices.
     Crack claws but leave whole.

SAUCE

2	teaspoons canola oil	1	teaspoon fresh sage leaves,
2	tablespoons olive oil		chopped
¼	cup shallots, coarsely chopped		coarsely ground black pepper
2	cloves garlic, minced	1	tablespoon white wine vinegar
4	anchovies, chopped	½	cup sour cream ("lite" if
1	tablespoon Dijon mustard		preferred)
1	tablespoon tomato paste		Lemon and rosemary for
¼	cup dry sherry		garnish

1.   Heat oil in a saucepan, add shallots and garlic. Do not brown. Add
tomato paste and mustard. Stir and cook over low heat for 8 minutes.
2.   Add other ingredients except sour cream. Cook for 10 minutes, then
add sour cream and lobster. Heat very gently for 10 minutes.
3.   Place mixture in a ceramic bowl, cool and refrigerate.
4.   Serve cold. Arrange on a platter. Fill tail shell with mixture, arrange
claws and lemon slices around tail. Garnish with fresh rosemary.

Insalata di Scampi
Shrimp Salad
Serves 4

1   pound unshelled medium-size shrimp

½   cup extra virgin olive oil

½   cup fresh lemon juice

2   garlic cloves, pressed

Salt and freshly ground black pepper

1.   Bring 2 quarts of water to a boil. Drop in the shrimp and continue to simmer for 2 to 3 minutes. Drain the shrimp and let them cool. Shell and devein the shrimp and refrigerate until ready to use.

2.   Mix together the remaining ingredients.

3.   Arrange the shrimp on a cold serving plate and pour some of the dressing over them, or serve it separately as a dipping sauce.

Scampi con Prosciutto e Pesto
Grilled Shrimp with Prosciutto and Pesto
Serves 4

If you don't have time to make your own, you can buy very good pesto in the super market these days.

12	shrimp, 16-20 count, or larger	1	lemon, sliced
12	slices of prosciutto, sliced very thin	½	lemon, juice of
1	cup Pesto, page 119	1	tablespoon butter
¼	cup dry white wine	2	tablespoon olive oil
			Salt and pepper to taste

1.   Clean and devein shrimp, leave tails on and butterfly. Open shrimp and spread with ½ teaspoon of Pesto. Bring halves together and wrap with prosciutto.

2.   Place shrimp in a shallow pan with butter and oil. Broil on one side for 2 minutes.

3.   Turn, add wine and lemon juice. Cook for 2 minutes more. Do not overcook. Remove when shrimp are still tender to touch. Garnish with lemon slices.

Ostriche al Gianni
Broiled Oysters
Serves 2 to 6

24	fresh oysters (Wellfleet oysters if you can find them)	½	cup fresh grated Parmigiano
½	cup Pesto (page 119)	1	cup fresh bread crumbs
		2	tablespoons olive oil

1.   Preheat the oven to 450 degrees.

2.   Rinse and open the oysters, leaving them on the half shell and being careful to keep their juices in the shell.

3.   Place the oysters on a baking sheet. Balance them on each other if necessary to keep the juices from spilling out.

4.   Top each oyster with ½ teaspoon of Pesto and a sprinkle of Parmigiano. Mix the bread crumbs with the oil. Place 1 teaspoon of the bread crumb mixture on each oyster.

5.   Bake or broil the oysters until the crumbs are golden brown.

Calamari Piccanti
Squid with Anchovies and Lemon
Serves 4

12	squid, cleaned	1	cup heavy cream
8	tablespoons butter	4	teaspoons fresh lemon juice
8	anchovy fillets, rinsed and dried		Salt and freshly ground black pepper
4	tablespoons dry white wine	4	lemon slices

1.   Slice the squid into ¼-inch-thick rings. Leave the tentacles whole.

2.   Melt the butter in a skillet. Add the anchovy fillets to the butter and mash them with a fork to dissolve them. Add the squid to the pan. Raise the heat to moderate and sauté for 5 minutes. Add the wine and let it reduce for a moment. Add the cream, raise the heat and reduce the sauce for 1 minute.

3.   Remove the squid to a warm serving dish.

4.   Add the lemon juice and salt and pepper to taste to the sauce and continue to reduce it until it is slightly thickened.

5.   Pour the sauce over the squid and serve garnished with the lemon slices.

Aringa Marinata
Marinated Herring

Dijon mustard
Maionese (page 265)
Lemon juice
Pinch of cayenne pepper

Pickled herring, cut into ¼-inch-thick slices
Romaine or Boston lettuce
Lemon slices

1.   Mix 2 parts mustard and one part maionese. Add a squeeze of lemon juice and a pinch of cayenne pepper and mix well.
2.   Add the herring to the sauce and toss well.
3.   Serve the herring on a bed of lettuce. Garnish with lemon slices.
4.   One portion would be one whole herring fillet.

Carpaccio di Salmone
Sliced Raw Salmon
Serves 8

1½	pounds salmon fillet, skinned, very fresh	2	tablespoon sour cream	
¾	cup green and black olive mix (store-bought)	1	tablespoon capers	
4	tablespoon Dijon mustard		Fresh black pepper	
1½	tablespoon horseradish	8	large lemon wedges	

1. With a very sharp knife, slice salmon paper thin.
2. Arrange on 8 plates. Make a mound of olive mix in center.
3. In a bowl mix mustard, horseradish, sour cream and capers. Drizzle over salmon. Garnish with lemon wedges.

Salmone Affumicato
Smoked Salmon

Smoked salmon
Romaine or Boston lettuce
Horseradish
Heavy cream

Freshly ground black pepper
Whole capers, rinsed
Bermuda onion, sliced into
thin rounds

1.   Slice the smoked salmon on the bias in ⅛-inch-thick slices.
2.   Line a dish with romaine or Boston lettuce. Arrange the slices of salmon on the lettuce.
3.   Beat together the heavy cream and horseradish to make a thick sauce. Season with freshly ground black pepper. Pour a little of this sauce over the salmon slices.
4.   Sprinkle whole capers over the salmon. Finally, arrange thin slices of Bermuda onion over the salmon.
5.   One portion would be 3 to 4 ounces of salmon.

Cannellini con Tonno
White Beans and Tuna
Seves 4

1	pound cannellini beans, washed	¼	teaspoon white pepper
1	cup olive oil	2	bay leaves
6	garlic cloves, crushed and peeled	1	cup white wine or dry vermouth
2	teaspoons salt	2	cans Italian tuna in oil

1.   Place beans in a stock pot with 8 cups of water and ½ cup of olive oil, bay leaves, garlic and salt and pepper. Bring to a boil. Reduce heat, add wine.
2.   When beans are soft, not broken, remove from heat and let cool.
3.   Place the tuna in a bowl. Break up into small pieces. Toss with beans and remaining olive oil. Garnish with a fresh herb.

Carpaccio di Tonno
Raw Tuna with Anchovies
Serves 6 to 8

1½	pounds tuna, sushi grade		Juice of 1 lemon
16	anchovy fillets, chopped coarse	1	lemon, sliced
½	cup virgin olive oil	1	small bunch of Italian flat-leaf parsley
16	green olives, slivered or sliced		

1.   Slice tuna paper thin and arrange on a serving platter. Place anchovies in center, surround with olives. Pour lemon juice and oil over all. Garnish with parsley and lemon slices.

MINESTRE E BRODI
Soups and Stocks

One night a large group of people was having dinner at the restaurant. Varujan Boghosian came in and ordered champagne for everyone in the party. When they had finished eating, he ordered after-dinner drinks for them all. He assured Ciro that he needn't worry about the check. When the waitress presented him with the bill, he simply ate it.

Minestrone con Fagiole e Salsiccia
Minestrone with Beans and Sausages
Serves 6

1	cup dried cannellini beans or chickpeas, sorted and rinsed
¼	cup olive oil
4	Italian sweet sausages
4	garlic cloves, finely chopped
1	onion, chopped
2	carrots, cut into ¼-inch-thick slices
2	celery stalks, thickly cut on the diagonal
2	teaspoons dried thyme
1	bay leaf
1	teaspoon dried oregano
1	teaspoon chopped fresh rosemary leaves
½	teaspoon fennel seeds, crushed
½	cup dry red wine
5	cups veal stock (page 64)
2	small zucchini, cut into ½-inch pieces
1	sweet green pepper, cut into ¹/2-inch pieces
½	pound plum tomatoes, peeled, seeded and coarsely chopped
2	tablespoons tomato paste
	Salt and freshly ground black pepper
¼	pound ditalini
½	cup Pesto (page 119), optional
	Freshly grated Parmigiano

1.   Soak the beans overnight in water to cover. Drain them and cover with fresh water. Cover the pot and bring to a boil, then lower the heat and cook the beans for 45 minutes to 2 hours (the chickpeas will take the longer time to cook).

2.   Heat the oil in a heavy saucepan. Add the whole sausages, and brown them on all sides. Remove the sausages and set them aside. Add the garlic, onion, carrot and celery to the pan. Sauté until the vegetables are tender. Add the herbs, wine and stock. Bring to a boil. Add the zucchini, green pepper, tomatoes, tomato paste and the cooked, drained beans. Slice the sausage into ¼-inch-thick rounds and add them to the soup. Simmer for 20 minutes.

3.   While the soup is cooking, cook the ditalini in salted boiling water until it is very al dente. Drain the ditalini and add it to the soup. You may not have to add all the ditalini; it should not overpower the other ingredients. Season with salt and pepper to taste. Continue to cook the soup for 10 minutes more.

4.   If desired, stir in the Pesto just before serving. Serve with freshly grated Parmigiano.

Zuppa di Ceci e Spinaci
Chick Pea and Spinach Soup
Serves 6

2	tablespoons olive oil	1	quart defatted chicken stock (page 65)
1	large onion, chopped fine		
3	large cloves garlic, pressed	½	cup fresh basil, chopped
3	cups canned ceci (chick peas)		Salt and pepper
1	cup tomato pulp	1	pound package spinach, stemmed and washed
5	quarts water		

1.   Heat oil in a soup pot. Add onions and garlic. Simmer until onions are soft.

2.   Add ceci and tomatoes and cook for 10 minutes.

3.   Add water and stock, bring to boil. Reduce heat and add basil and salt and pepper. Let simmer for 20 minutes.

4.   Add spinach, cover and remove from heat. May be garnished with seasoned croutons.

Zuppa di Fave e Cavi
Fava Beans and Cabbage
Serves 4 to 6

1 cup Savoy cabbage, shredded
½ cup celery, chopped fine
1 medium onion, finely chopped
2 tablespoons basil, finely chopped, or 1 teaspoon dried
6 cups water
¾ pound ground chicken or turkey breast

1 egg white (or Egg Beaters)
1 cup canned fava beans
1 medium potato, diced
1½ tablespoons parsley, finely chopped
½ lemon, juice of
½ cup tubettini
Parsley for garnish

1.   In a soup pot put cabbage, celery, onion, basil and water. Bring to a boil and simmer for 1 hour.

2.   Mix the ground chicken with egg white, salt and pepper. Form balls about the size of a nickel.

3.   Add the potatoes, fava beans and chicken balls to the pot. Cook for 15 to 20 minutes.

4.   Add lemon juice, salt, pepper and parsley. Cook tubettini separately. Add to soup bowls individually. Garnish with more parsley.

Minestra di Fagioli e Escarole
Bean and Escarole Soup
Serves 6

2	tablespoons olive oil	1	bay leaf
1	large onion, chopped fine	1	teaspoon thyme
2	cloves garlic, pressed	1	small head of escarole
2	tablespoons tomato paste		(chickory), washed
2	carrots, diced	1	cup tubettini or orzo,
2	stalks celery, chopped fine		cooked al dente
6	cups water	½	cup grated Romano
1	cup chicken stock, defatted		
8	cups cannellini beans		
	(home-cooked or canned)		

1.   Heat oil in a large pot (8 quart). Add onions. When onions glaze add tomato paste and garlic. Simmer for 5 minutes. Add water and bring to boil. Reduce heat to simmer.

2.   Add other ingredients except pasta and escarole. Cook for 20 minutes. Add escarole. Cover and cook for ten minutes on low heat.

3.   Meanwhile, in another pot cook the pasta. Add pasta to soup just before serving. Garnish with Romano.

Minestra di Lentichie
Lentil Soup
Serves 6

¼	cup olive oil	1	bay leaf
2	ounces prosciùtto, untrimmed and in 1 piece	½	cup dry red wine
		6	cups veal stock (page 64)
1	onion, finely chopped	2	tomatoes, peeled, seeded and chopped
1	carrot, finely chopped		
1	celery stalk, finely chopped	1	tablespoon dry mustard
3	garlic cloves, finely chopped	1	tablespoon red wine vinegar
3	cups lentils, sorted and rinsed		Salt and freshly ground
2	teaspoons dried thyme		black pepper
1	teaspoon ground cumin		

1. Heat the olive oil in a large heavy saucepan. Add the prosciutto, onion, carrot, celery and garlic. Sauté, stirring occasionally, until the vegetables are soft.

2. Add the lentils, herbs, wine and stock. Cover the pot and bring to a boil. Lower the heat and cook slowly for 1 to 2 hours, or until the lentils are tender. If the lentils start to get dry, add more stock.

3. Add the remaining ingredients to the soup. Cook for 15 minutes longer. Serve immediately.

4. For a variation, ⅓ to ½ of the soup may be puréed and then added back to the whole lentils. Garnish with a dollop of sour cream and extra chopped tomatoes.

Minestra di Zucchini con Pomodori e Basilico
Zucchini Soup with Tomatoes and Basil
Serves 6

4	tablespoons butter	4	cups chicken stock (page 65)
1	onion, finely chopped	4	large ripe tomatoes, peeled,
1	small carrot, finely chopped		seeded and chopped
½	celery stalk, finely chopped	6	fresh basil leaves, chopped
4	garlic cloves, finely chopped		Salt and freshly ground
4	medium-size zucchini,		black pepper
	chopped	½	cup light cream, at room
2	teaspoons dried thyme		temperature
1	bay leaf		Fresh basil leaves for garnish
½	cup dry white wine		

1.   Melt the butter in a heavy saucepan. Add the onion, carrot, celery and garlic and sauté the vegetables until they are tender.

2.   Add the zucchini and herbs, stir, and sauté for 15 minutes.

3.   Add the wine and stock to the pot and bring to a boil. Cover the pot and cook for 35 to 40 minutes.

4.   Remove the soup from the heat and purée it in a food processor or blender. Pour the purée into the top of a double boiler over simmering water. Add the chopped tomatoes and basil. Season with salt and pepper to taste.

5.   Pour a ladleful of the soup into the cream and then pour the mixture back into the soup. Heat slowly. Garnish each serving with fresh basil leaves.

Minestra di Finocchio
Fennel Soup
Serves 6

4	tablespoons butter	½	cup dry white wine
1	leek, white part only, finely chopped	4	cups chicken stock (page 65)
1	medium-size carrot, finely chopped	½ to ¾	cup light cream, at room temperature
3	garlic cloves, finely chopped		Salt and freshly ground black pepper
1	teaspoon dried thyme	2	tablespoons anise-flavored liqueur, such as Anisette,
1	bay leaf		Pernod, Sambuca, etc.
2	heads fresh fennel		

1.   Melt the butter in a heavy saucepan. Add the leek, carrot and garlic, and sauté until the vegetables are tender. Add the thyme and bay leaf.

2.   Remove the green parts and the stem from the fennel bulbs. (Reserve these to use in making vegetable broth (page 66) Coarsely chop the bulbs and add them to the pan. Sauté for 10 minutes.

3.   Add the wine and chicken stock and bring to a boil. Lower the heat and simmer, covered, for 30 to 40 minutes.

4.   Remove the soup from the heat and purée it in a blender or food processor. Pour the purée into the top of a double boiler over simmering water. Pour a ladleful of the soup into the cream, and then pour the mixture back into the soup. Season with salt and pepper to taste. Stir in the liqueur and heat slowly until hot.

Minestra di Cavolifiore
Cauliflower Soup

Simply substitute one head of cauliflower, flowerets only, for the fennel.

Crema di Funghi con Zafferano
Mushroom Soup with Saffron
Serves 6

4	tablespoons butter	½	cup dry white wine
1	onion, finely chopped	4	cups veal stock (page 64)
1	carrot, finely chopped	¼	cup cream sherry
1	celery stalk, finely chopped	2	pinches of saffron threads
3	garlic cloves, finely chopped	½ to ¾	cup light cream, at
1	pound fresh mushrooms,		room temperature
	cleaned and sliced		Salt and freshly ground
2	teaspoons dried thyme		black pepper
1	bay leaf		

1.   Melt the butter in a heavy saucepan. Add the onion, carrot, celery and garlic and sauté until the vegetables are tender. Add the mushrooms, thyme and bay leaf, stir, and sauté for 10 minutes.

2.   Add the wine and stock and bring to a boil. Cover the pan, lower the heat and cook for 30 to 40 minutes.

3.   Remove the soup from the heat and purée it in a blender or food processor. Pour the purée into the top of a double boiler over simmering water. Add the sherry and saffron and cook for 10 minutes.

4.   Pour a ladleful of the soup into the cream, and then pour the mixture back into the soup. Season with salt and pepper to taste.

NOTE: Dried porcini mushrooms that have been soaked, can be added to the soup for a more complex flavor.

Zuppa di Zucchini Machinate
Creamed Zucchini Soup
Serves 6

8   cups chicken stock, defatted
1   tablespoon minced Italian flat parsley
2   tablespoons fresh basil
1   cup diced potatoes

3   cups diced zucchini
     salt and fresh black pepper
½   cup non-fat non-dairy creamer (such as Farm Rich brand)

1.   Boil stock, add all ingredients except zucchini and cream.
2.   When potatoes are almost cooked, add zucchini. Cook for 10 minutes.
3.   Pour soup into blender and purée. Add non-dairy creamer.

NOTE: Can be garnished with seasoned croutons and fresh basil.

Purè di Pomodoro con Pesto
Purée of Tomato Soup with Pesto
Serves 6

4	tablespoons butter	1	teaspoon dried oregano
4	garlic cloves, finely chopped	½	cup dry white wine
1	onion, finely chopped	4	cups chicken stock (page 65)
1	small carrot, finely chopped	½	cup light cream, at room
1½	pounds ripe tomatoes,		temperature
	peeled, seeded and chopped	½	cup Pesto (page 119)
2	teaspoons dried thyme		Salt and freshly ground
1	bay leaf		black pepper

1.   Melt the butter in a heavy saucepan. Add the garlic, onions and carrot, and sauté until the vegetables are tender. Add the tomatoes, thyme, bay leaf and oregano. Stir and cook for 5 minutes.

2.   Add the wine and chicken stock and bring to a boil. Cover the pot, lower the heat and cook for 30 minutes.

3.   Remove the soup from the heat and purée it in a food processor. Pour the purée into the top of a double boiler over simmering water. Pour a ladleful of the soup into the cream, and then pour the mixture back into the soup. Swirl in the Pesto, and season the soup with salt and pepper to taste. Heat slowly.

NOTE: This soup may also be chilled and served as a cold summertime soup.

Straciatella
Egg Drop Soup
Serves 4

6	cups chicken broth, defatted	5	egg whites or 1 carton Egg Beaters, beaten
2	cups fresh spinach or Swiss chard, washed, stemmed and chopped coarsely	1	tablespoon grated lemon rind
			Salt and pepper
		1	tablespoon grated Parmigiano

1.   Bring broth to boil, add spinach. Lower heat, cook for 2 minutes.
2.   Beat egg whites with salt, pepper, lemon rind and cheese. Dribble into simmering broth. Stir gently and turn off heat. Let sit for 5 minutes before serving.

Zuppa di Capesante e Cozze
Soup with Scallops and Mussels
Serves 8

2	tablespoons olive oil	1	leek, julienned and washed thoroughly
1	tablespoon canola oil		
1	medium onion, finely chopped	3 or 4	pounds fish racks* (haddock, flounder or cod)
3	cloves garlic, pressed		
3	tablespoons parsley, chopped fine	2	celery hearts, coarsely chopped
½	cup dry white wine	24	mussels
½	cup dry sherry	1	pound sea scallops, cut in quarters
8	cups water		Fresh rosemary sprigs
1	bay leaf		

1.   Make fish stock: Put in all ingredients except scallops, mussels and celery hearts. Bring to a boil and then simmer for 30 minutes.
2.   Strain out solids and return broth to pot. Add celery, cook over low heat 10 minutes.
3.   Add mussels and when they open, add scallops. Remove from heat and cover. Garnish with fresh rosemary.

* Racks are the skeletons of fish left after filleting.

Brodo di Pollo con Uove
Chicken Broth with Egg
Serves 8

1	3½-to 4-pound chicken, cut in pieces	2	bay leaves
1	large onion, chopped	1	teaspoon thyme
3	medium carrots, chopped		Black pepper and salt
2	stalks of celery, chopped	2	egg whites or Egg Beaters
		1	tablespoon grated Parmigiano

1.   Wash chicken. Place in a large pot with 4 quarts of water. Bring to boil. Remove scum. Reduce heat and add vegetables and seasonings.

2.   When meat pulls from bone turn off heat and let soup cool. Discard bones and skin. Strain soup; save the vegetables. Place soup in refrigerator.

3.   When fat congeals remove it and return pot to heat. Add diced chicken and vegetables, let simmer for 10 minutes.

4.   Beat egg whites or Egg Beaters with Parmigiano and black pepper, Add to hot soup. Garnish with fresh parsley.

NOTE: Another version of this—Eliminate the eggs and purée the soup in a processor. Garnish with croutons and Parmigiano.

Zuppa di Bue e Polpette
Beef Soup with Small Meatballs
Serves 6 to 8

1	pound lean beef or veal	10	cups beef stock (page 63)
2	egg whites, beaten (or Egg Beaters)	½	cup long grain rice
1	tablespoon grated lemon zest	½	cup dry sherry
1	tablespoon finely minced parsley	8	cups Swiss chard, coarsely chopped
	Salt, pepper and a pinch of nutmeg		Salt and pepper
			Watercress for garnish

1. Combine the ground meat, salt, pepper, nutmeg, lemon zest, egg whites and parsley. Mix well. Form by hand into small meat balls, about the size of a nickel.
2. Bring broth to a boil. Add rice, cook for 10 minutes. Add wine and meatballs. Cook over medium heat for 15 minutes, then add Swiss chard and cook another 10 minutes. Garnish with watercress.

Brodo di Carne
Beef Stock
Yield: 5 Quarts

7	pounds beef bones, chopped	1	medium-size carrot, peeled and cut into quarters
4	ounces (½ cup) lard or pork fat	2	large cloves garlic, unpeeled
2	pounds beef chuck or trimmings	7	quarts cold water
1	medium-size onion, peeled and cut into quarters	½	cup tomato puree cup dry red wine
1	large celery stalk, cut into quarters	½	teaspoon salt
		1	bay leaf
		¼	teaspoon crushed black peppercorns
		½	bunch parsley sprigs (stems and leaves), washed

1. Preheat the oven to 400 degrees.
2. Rinse the bones in cold water and pat them dry with paper towels.
3. Put the lard in a roasting pan and melt it in the oven. Add the bones and beef and brown them lightly, stirring occasionally. Add the vegetables and brown them along with the beef bones.
4. Remove the pan from the oven and drain off the fat. Transfer the contents of the roasting pan to a large stock pot and add the cold water. Cover the pot and bring the water to a boil over high heat. Skim off any foam or fat and add the remaining ingredients. Bring the stock back to a boil and then lower the heat to keep the stock at a simmer. Let it cook for 3 hours. Skim the surface of the stock as necessary.
5. After 3 hours, strain the stock through a fine mesh strainer. Discard the bones, etc., and let the stock cool. If a clearer stock is desired, line the strainer with cheesecloth.

NOTE: The stock can be stored tightly covered in the refrigerator for several days or it can be frozen in pint or quart containers and used as needed.

Brodo di Vitello
Veal Stock
Yield: 5 Quarts

6	pounds veal bones, cut up	½	bunch parsley sprigs (stems and leaves), washed
6	quarts cold water		
1	cup dry white wine	½	teaspoon dried thyme
1	large onion, cut in half	1	bay leaf
2	celery stalks, cut in half	½	teaspoon crushed black peppercorns
1	whole tomato, seeded		
1	small carrot, peeled		

1.   Rinse the bones in cold water.

2.   Place the bones in a large stock pot and add the cold water (see Note). Cover the pot and bring the water to a boil. Skim off any foam or fat that rises to the surface.

3.   Add the remaining ingredients and return the stock to a boil. Lower the heat and simmer the stock for 2 hours. Skim the surface of the stock as necessary.

4.   Strain the stock through a fine mesh strainer and discard the bones, etc. Let the stock cool. Store in pint or quart containers in the refrigerator or freezer.

NOTE: Veal trimmings may be added to the stock for extra flavor.

Brodo di Pollo
Chicken Stock
Yield: 5 Quarts

6	pounds chicken bones, or		2	celery stalks, cut in half
	1 3-pound whole chicken		1	teaspoon dried thyme
6	quarts cold water		½	bunch parsley sprigs (leaves
1	cup dry white wine			and stems), washed
1	large onion, peeled and cut		1	bay leaf
	in half		¼	teaspoon crushed black
1	medium-size carrot, peeled			peppercorns
	and cut in half			

1.   Rinse the bones or chicken in cold water, put them in a large stock pot and add the cold water (see Note). Cover the pot and bring the water to a boil over high heat. Skim off any foam or fat that rises to the surface.

2.   Add the remaining ingredients and return the stock to a boil. Lower the heat and simmer for 2 hours. Skim the surface as necessary.

3.   Strain the stock through a fine mesh strainer and discard the bones, etc. Let the stock cool and store in pint or quart containers in the refrigerator or freezer.

NOTE: For a darker, richer stock, the bones and vegetables may be browned in 2 to 4 ounces (¼ to ½ cup) fat in a 400-degree oven before being added to the stock pot.

Brodo di Legumi
Vegetable Stock
Yield: 5 Quarts

¼ cup olive oil
1   large onion, coarsely chopped
2   large celery stalks, coarsely chopped
2   fennel stalks, coarsely chopped
1   zucchini, coarsely chopped

1   garlic clove, unpeeled
6   quarts cold water
1   cup dry white wine
1   bay leaf
1   teaspoon dried thyme
1   small bunch parsley sprigs (stems and leaves), washed

1.   Heat the oil in a large stock pot. Add the vegetables and sauté until they are golden. Add the remaining ingredients, cover, and bring to a boil. Lower the heat and simmer the stock for 1 hour.
2.   Strain the stock through a fine mesh strainer and let cool. Store in pint or quart containers in the refrigerator or freezer.

Brodo di Pesce
Fish Stock
Yield: 5 Quarts

5	pounds fish bones, heads and tails	1	garlic clove, unpeeled
5	quarts cold water	1	bay leaf
1	cup dry white wine	5	parsley sprigs (leaves and stems), washed
1	small onion, peeled	1	teaspoon salt
1	celery stalk		

1.   If you are using the heads from round fish (as opposed to flat fish, such as flounder), remove the gills and discard so that they will not release blood into the stock.

2.   Put the bones, heads and tails into a large stock pot and add the cold water (see Note). Cover the pot and bring the water to a boil over high heat. Skim off any foam or fat that rises to the surface.

3.   Add the remaining ingredients and bring to a boil. Lower the heat and simmer the stock for 30 minutes.

4.   Strain the stock through a fine mesh strainer. Discard the bones, etc. and let cool. Store in small containers in the refrigerator or freezer.

NOTE: Shrimp shells can also be added to the stock for extra flavor.

PASTE E SALSE

Things were still in their infancy when I made my first visit to Ciro & Sal's. The place had only been open for a month, but I was just two weeks old myself and didn't mind the chaos.

As a street urchin, I spent my mornings selling shells on Commercial Street and diving for coins that tourists tossed from MacMillan Wharf. Early each afternoon, I would slip into the kitchen at Ciro's— the restaurant was not yet open—and nonchalantly slice myself a thick hunk of Italian bread. I would present it to the man himself, who ceremoniously dunked it in his giant, simmering pot of tomato sauce and returned it to me. No urchin ever ate better.

Some evenings, long after I should have been in bed, my mother took me to Ciro's after closing time. Sitting on padded kegs and listening to the proprietors and their iconoclastic coterie discuss life and art while Italian arias played in the background, I learned great lessons early.

Many people you've heard of find their way to Ciro's, but I only heard the kitchen hush once. That was the night a waiter brought in an order for our best steak. "Make it a good one," he said. "It's for John Wayne. "

In the ensuing years, I have shared Ciro's magic with appreciative guests throughout the hemisphere. A Sandinista comandante is the latest to ask for the sauce recipe.

STEPHEN KINZER
Correspondent, *The New York Times*
Author, *Blood of Brothers*

Spaghetti al Burro e Formaggio
Spaghetti with Butter and Cheese
Serves 4 to 6

1	pound spaghetti	4	tablespoons finely chopped
12	tablespoons sweet butter		fresh parsley leaves
1	teaspoon pressed garlic	3	tablespoons freshly grated
2	tablespoons finely chopped		Pecorino Romano
	fresh basil leaves		Freshly ground black pepper

1. Cook the spaghetti in salted boiling water until it is al dente.
2. While the spaghetti is cooking, melt the butter in a skillet. Add the garlic and lower the heat.
3. Drain the spaghetti and add it to the butter and garlic in the skillet. Toss quickly. Add the remaining ingredients and toss again. Serve at once.

Spaghetti con Alio, Olio e Limone
Spaghetti with Garlic, Oil and Lemon
Serves 4 to 6

1	pound spaghetti		Salt and freshly ground
⅔	cup extra virgin olive oil		black pepper
6	garlic cloves, finely chopped	1	lemon, quartered

1.   Cook the spaghetti in salted boiling water until it is al dente.

2.   While the spaghetti is cooking, heat the oil in a skillet and sauté the garlic over very low heat until it becomes a rich golden brown.

3.   Drain the spaghetti and add it to the oil and garlic in the skillet. Add the salt and pepper and toss again. Serve immediately garnished with the lemon wedges.

Spaghettini alla Primavera
Spaghettini Genoa Style
Serves 6

1	pound spaghettini, cooked al dente	4	tablespoons fresh basil, chopped
2	pounds fresh, ripe tomatoes	5	tablespoons olive oil
1	pound red onions, thinly sliced		Salt and pepper

1.   Pierce tomatoes with a fork. Immerse in boiling water for 2 minutes, then peel and seed. Chop in large chunks.

2.   Mix with onions, basil and olive oil and let stand for 30 minutes or more. Toss with hot pasta and garnish with a sprig of basil.

NOTE: This is a light, fast summer lunch or supper. Great when tomatoes from the garden are ripe and juicy!

Spaghetti con Funghi
Spaghetti with Mushrooms
Serves 4 to 6

4	tablespoons butter	1½	cups Ragù (page 117)
1½	cups thinly sliced mushrooms	1	pound spaghetti or linguine
2	teaspoons pressed garlic		Freshly grated Parmigiano
4	tablespoons dry white wine		

1.   Melt the butter in a skillet. Add the mushrooms, and sauté them for 1 minute. Add the garlic and wine and continue to cook until the mushrooms are tender. Add the Ragù to the pan and heat slowly.

2.   Cook the spaghetti in salted boiling water until it is al dente. Drain the spaghetti and transfer it to a warm serving bowl. Pour the sauce over the spaghetti and toss rapidly. Serve immediately with the grated Parmigiano.

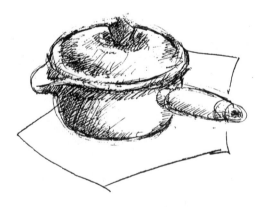

Spaghetti con Pepperoni
Spaghetti with Peppers
Serves 4 to 6

1	pound spaghetti	2	teaspoons pressed garlic
4	sweet green peppers	1½	cups Ragù (page 117)
3	tablespoons olive oil		Freshly grated Parmigiano

1. Preheat oven to 400 degrees.

2. Wash and dry the peppers. Put the oil and garlic in a baking pan and roll the peppers in the oil, being sure to coat the peppers completely. Bake, uncovered, until the skins blister, turning them occasionally. Remove the peppers from the oven and put them in a paper bag; close the bag tightly. Let the peppers steam for 5 minutes; then peel, core and seed them under cold running water. Slice the peppers into ½ inch-wide strips.

3. Heat the Ragù slowly. Add the peppers to the sauce and continue heating for 10 minutes.

4. While the sauce is cooking, cook the spaghetti in salted boiling water until it is al dente.

5. Drain the spaghetti and transfer it to a warm serving bowl. Pour the sauce over the pasta, toss quickly and serve immediately with grated Parmigiano.

*S*al and Josephine spent their honeymoon at his parents' birthplace, an island off the coast of Naples. It was in Foria, Ischia, that they tasted an unusual spaghetti served during Lent. Back in Provincetown, he and Ciro tried to re-create the spaghetti with a sauce made of anchovies. They continued to experiment, adding new ingredients until they finally created what is now known as Spaghetti alla Foriana, still a house favorite to this day.

I write during Lent, 1986. I am reminded of one of my favorite dishes anywhere, a traditional Italian Lenten dish called Spaghetti alla Foriana, which I first encountered at "Ciro and Sal's" decades ago. I still order it there, decades later, along with whatever else pleases me. The restaurant's basic character is that of a civilized "bistro," the kind of restaurant that most artists love...

Apart from his lovable restaurant, Ciro Cozzi deserves the gratitude of the art community in Provincetown for his continual generosity, good will and empathy toward the arts which has manifested itself over many years in scores of ways, large and small. What a marvelous friend and neighbor!

ROBERT MOTHERWELL

Spaghetti alla Foriana
Spaghetti with Nuts, Raisins and Anchovies
Serves 4 to 6

1	pound spaghetti	½	cup dark raisins
¾	cup extra virgin olive oil	1	teaspoon dried oregano
4	garlic cloves, finely chopped		Pinch of hot red pepper
12	anchovy fillets, rinsed and dried		flakes
½	cup walnuts, broken into quarters		Pinch of freshly ground black pepper
¼	cup pine nuts, lightly toasted	4	tablespoons finely chopped fresh parsley leaves

1.   Cook the spaghetti in salted boiling water until it is al dente.

2.   While the spaghetti is cooking, heat the oil in a deep skillet. Add the garlic and 9 of the anchovy fillets and sauté over low heat until the garlic is golden and the anchovies have dissolved (mash them with a fork). Add the walnuts, pine nuts, raisins, oregano, and black and red pepper and simmer for 4 minutes.

3.   Drain the spaghetti and add it to the anchovy mixture in the pan. Add 3 tablespoons of the parsley and toss quickly.

4.   Transfer the pasta to a warm serving bowl and garnish with the remaining anchovy fillets and parsley.

Spaghetti alla Carbonara
Spaghetti with Pancetta, Eggs and Cream
Serves 4 to 6

½   pound pancetta, diced
3   large eggs, beaten
½   cup heavy cream
2   tablespoons freshly grated
     Parmigiano

1   teaspoon finely chopped
     fresh parsley leaves
     Freshly ground black pepper
1   pound spaghetti

1.   Fry the pancetta in a large skillet until it is slightly crispy but not tough. Drain the fat from the pan.

2.   Beat together the eggs, milk, cheese, parsley and black pepper.

3.   Cook the spaghetti in salted boiling water until it is al dente. Drain the spaghetti and add it to the pancetta in the pan. Add the egg mixture. Cook briefly over very low heat, tossing to coat all the spaghetti with the egg. Do not overcook; the sauce should remain creamy.

4.   Serve immediately with extra grated Parmigiano.

$\mathcal{F}$or many years when prostitution was legal in Italy (it was outlawed in 1958), the busy Neapolitan prostitutes made Spaghetti alla Puttanesca. Some say this was because the sauce could be prepared quickly; others say it was because the strong aroma lured potential customers. Both could be right.

Spaghetti alla Puttanesca
Spaghetti of the Whores
Serves 4 to 6

1	pound spaghetti	2	ounces anchovy fillets, rinsed, drained and chopped (about 16 fillets)
¼	cup olive oil		
3	garlic cloves, finely chopped		
1	28-ounce can plum tomatoes, drained, seeded and coarsely chopped	½	dried chili pepper, finely chopped
		1	teaspoon dried basil
1	tablespoon capers, rinsed and drained	1	teaspoon dried oregano
		2	tablespoons finely chopped Fresh parsley
15	pitted black olives, thinly sliced		

1.   Heat the oil in a large saucepan. Add the garlic and sauté until it is golden. Do not burn.

2.   Add all the remaining ingredients except the parsley, and cook slowly for 15 minutes.

3.   While the sauce is simmering, cook the spaghetti in salted boiling water until it is al dente.

4.   Drain the spaghetti and transfer it to a warm serving bowl. Pour the sauce over the spaghetti and toss quickly. Sprinkle with the chopped parsley. Serve immediately.

NOTE: This spaghetti is wonderful with calamari (squid). Clean one dozen squid and slice them into thin rings. Use the tentacles also but keep them whole. Add the squid to the sauce and cook until tender (about 15 minutes). Pour over the cooked spaghetti and toss quickly.

Spaghetti con Salsiccia
Spaghetti with Sausages
Serves 4 to 6

8	Italian sweet sausages	1	pound spaghetti
½	cup water		Freshly grated Parmigiano
1½	cups Ragù (page 117)		

1.   Preheat the oven to 400 degrees.

2.   Put the sausages in a baking pan just large enough to hold them in one layer. Add the water, cover with aluminum foil and bake until cooked, 20 to 30 minutes.

3.   Remove the sausages from the pan and add them to a saucepan with the Ragù. Heat slowly.

4.   Cook the spaghetti in salted boiling water until it is al dente. Drain the spaghetti and transfer it to a warm serving bowl. Pour most of the Ragù over the spaghetti and toss quickly. Serve the sausages in the remaining sauce on a separate dish. Serve immediately with the grated Parmigiano.

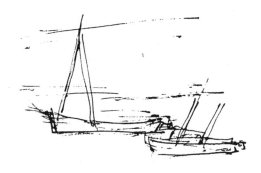

Pesce con Salsa di Pepperoni
Fish with Bell Pepper Sauce
Serves 6

This dish is open to improvisation, depending on what fish is fresh and plentiful and how many mouths there are to feed.

1	recipe Pepper Sauce (page 120)
1	pound any pasta—linguini, spaghettini, penne, or farfalle
½	pound fish per serving— flounder, cod or haddock

Fish stock or clam juice to barely cover fish
White wine
Savory, salt and pepper
Fresh chives, chopped, for garnish

1.   In a shallow pan place fish and cover with fish stock or clam juice. Add herbs and spices. Cook at low heat for 10 minutes.
2.   Add wine and simmer until fish is opaque and just done.
3.   Meanwhile, cook the pasta al dente. When pasta is cooked, drain.
4.   Break fish into bite size pieces, add fish liquid to Pepper Sauce and quickly heat together. Toss with pasta, garnish with chives.

Spaghetti con Vongole in Bianco
Spaghetti with Clams
Serves 4 to 6

32	cherrystone clams (about 8 pounds total weight)	½	teaspoon dried oregano
1	pound spaghetti or linguine	½	teaspoon hot red pepper flakes
⅔	cup olive oil	2	tablespoons finely chopped fresh parsley
5	garlic cloves, finely chopped		
1	tablespoon chopped fresh basil leaves		

1.   To facilitate opening the clams, place them on a tray and put them into a very hot oven for 2 minutes. Open the clams, remove the meat and reserve the juice. Cut each clam into two or three pieces.

2.   Cook the spaghetti in salted boiling water until it is al dente. While the spaghetti is cooking, heat the oil in a skillet. Add the garlic and sauté until it is golden. Add the reserved clam juice, basil, oregano and pepper flakes and bring to a boil. Add the clams and 1½ tablespoons of the parsley. Cook over moderate heat just until the clams are hot.

3.   Drain the spaghetti and transfer it to a warm serving bowl. Pour the clam sauce over the spaghetti and toss quickly. Sprinkle with the remaining parsley and serve immediately.

Linguini con Vongole e Acciughe
Linguini with Clams and Anchovies
Serves 6

1½	pounds linguini, cooked al dente	½	cup dry white wine
1½	dozen little neck clams	¼	cup chopped fresh basil
4	tablespoons olive oil	½	teaspoon dried rosemary, crushed
3	cloves garlic, finely chopped	3	tablespoons minced parsley
8	anchovies		Salt and pepper to taste

1.   Open clams over a bowl. Save liquid. Cut each clam in half.

2.   Sauté garlic in oil (do not brown), add anchovies, wine, clam liquid, and herbs. Simmer for 5 minutes. Add salt and pepper to taste. Turn off heat and add the clams. Toss with hot pasta.

Pasta all 'Abruzzese
Pasta with Seafood, Tomatoes and Herbs
Serves 4

¼	cup olive oil	½	pound boneless and skinless haddock or cod
3	garlic cloves, finely chopped		
1	onion, finely chopped	4	mussels, scrubbed and debearded
3	cups imported Italian plum tomatoes, peeled, seeded and chopped	8	shrimp, peeled and deveined
		4	littleneck clams, washed
½	cup fish stock (page 67)	2	squid, cleaned and cut into rings
2	tablespoons dry white wine		
1	tablespoon chopped fresh basil leaves	3	tablespoons finely chopped fresh parsley
¼	teaspoon hot red pepper flakes	1	pound spaghetti or linguine

1.   Heat the oil in a large saucepan. Add the garlic and onions and sauté until the onion is translucent.

2.   Add the tomatoes, stock, wine, basil and hot pepper flakes to the pan. Simmer for 20 minutes.

3.   Transfer 1 cup of this sauce to another saucepan and poach the haddock in it. Do not overcook the fish.

4.   At the same time, add the remaining seafood and 2 tablespoons of the parsley to the sauce. Cover and cook for 10 minutes, or until all the seafood is cooked. Leave the clams and mussels in their shells.

5.   While the seafood is cooking, cook the spaghetti in salted boiling water until it is al dente. Drain the spaghetti and transfer it to a warm serving bowl.

6.   Place the haddock in the center of the spaghetti and surround it with the other seafood. Pour the sauce over the spaghetti and sprinkle with the remaining parsley.

Pasta con Salsa di Noci
Pasta with Walnut Sauce
Serves 4 to 6

1   pound linguine or fettuccine
1   cup walnuts, chopped
⅓   cup blanched almonds, toasted and chopped
2   garlic cloves, chopped
2   tablespoons fresh marjoram, chopped
¼   cup fresh parsley, chopped
¼   cup fresh basil leaves, chopped
6   tablespoons whole milk ricotta

2   tablespoons freshly grated Pecorino Romano
½   cup extra virgin olive oil
     Salt and freshly ground black pepper
12 to 18 whole walnut halves, toasted
     Freshly grated Pecorino Romano

1.   Cook the pasta in salted boiling water until it is al dente.

2.   While the pasta is cooking, combine the remaining ingredients in a food processor or blender and blend until smooth. Heat the sauce over very low heat.

3.   Drain the pasta, leaving it slightly wet, and transfer it to a warm serving bowl. Add the walnut sauce and toss well. Do not add all of the sauce if there is too much; this should not be a heavy dish.

4.   Serve immediately with additional freshly grated Pecorino Romano and toasted whole walnuts—3 per serving.

     This sauce is also excellent with tortellini.

NOTE: If a slightly thinner or creamier sauce is desired, add a little heavy cream to the sauce as you heat it.

Linguini Fini con Lentiche
Thin Linguini with Lentils
Serves 6 to 8

1	pound thin linguini, cooked al dente	4	large cloves garlic, minced
10	ounces lentils, pre-soaked	2	tablespoons tomato paste
4	tablespoons olive oil	¼	teaspoon red pepper flakes
1	stick butter	½	teaspoon rosemary, crushed
2	carrots, finely chopped	1	tablespoon Dijon mustard
2	onions, finely chopped	½	cup dry sherry
1	medium fennel bulb, finely chopped		

1. Soak lentils in water to cover for ½ hour, then drain.
2. Heat olive oil and half the butter in a medium size sauce pan. Add the chopped vegetables, the lentils and all seasonings except the sherry. Add 5 cups water and simmer for ½ hour. Do not let lentils become mushy. Add sherry during last 5 minutes.
3. Toss hot linguini with remaining 4 tablespoons butter. Pour lentils over pasta.

NOTE: This is a robust dish, and meatless, too. Adding the sherry last preserves its subtle flavor.

Linguine alla Figlia
Linguine with Piquant Tomato Sauce
and Goat Cheese
Serves 4 to 6

3	tablespoons olive oil	1	teaspoon chopped fresh rosemary leaves
3	garlic cloves, finely chopped		
½	carrot, finely chopped	2	teaspoons chopped fresh parsley leaves
1	celery stalk, finely chopped		
1	small onion, finely chopped		Salt and freshly ground black pepper
2	anchovy fillets, rinsed, dried and chopped		Dash of red wine vinegar
8	sun-dried tomatoes, soaked for 30 minutes in tepid water, and then drained and rinsed		Pinch of hot red pepper flakes
¼	cup dry red wine	1	pound linguine
1	1-pound can imported Italian plum tomatoes	4	tablespoons butter, cut into small pieces and at room temperature (optional)
1	bay leaf	4	ounces mild goat cheese, broken up (optional)
1	teaspoon chopped fresh basil leaves		Freshly grated Parmigiano

1.   Heat the oil in a heavy saucepan. Add the garlic, carrot, celery and onion and sauté until the vegetables are tender. Add the anchovies and sun-dried tomatoes. Mash them with a fork until they dissolve.

2.   Pass the contents of the pan through a large mesh sieve (to remove the tomato skins). Return the purée to the pan and add the wine. Let the wine reduce to about 3 tablespoons.

3.   Pass the tomatoes through a sieve to remove the seeds. Add the tomatoes, bay leaf, basil, rosemary and parsley to the pan. Simmer over very low heat for 2 hours. Add the vinegar and hot pepper flakes. Season with salt and pepper.

4.   Cook the linguine in boiling salted water until it is al dente. Drain and transfer it to a warm serving bowl. If desired, add the butter and toss quickly to melt. Add the goat cheese and toss, then pour the sauce over the pasta (reserve ¼ cup) and toss again. Pour the remaining sauce on top.
5.   Serve immediately with freshly grated Parmigiano.

Linguine Estive
Summertime Linguine
Serves 4 to 6

1	pound linguine		Salt and freshly ground
¾	cup extra virgin olive oil		black pepper
4	garlic cloves, sliced	1	pound fresh mozzarella,
4	large ripe tomatoes, cut into		cut into small cubes and at
	¼-inch wedges		room temperature
10	fresh basil leaves, stems removed		

1.   Cook the linguine in boiling salted water until it is al dente.
2.   Heat the oil in a heavy skillet. Add the garlic and sauté until it is golden brown. Remove the garlic and discard. Lower the heat and add the tomatoes, basil, salt and pepper. Cook for 1 minute.
3.   Drain the linguine and transfer it to a warm serving bowl. Pour the sauce over the linguine and toss quickly but well. Add the mozzarella and toss again. Serve immediately.

Linguini con Melanzane
Linguini with Eggplant
Serves 6

1	pound linguini, cooked al dente	4	tablespoons fresh basil, chopped
2	medium eggplants, sliced ¼-inch thick		Red pepper flakes, salt and black pepper to taste
4	tablespoons olive oil	2	cups Marinara Sauce
1	clove garlic, minced		(page 116)
4	cups tomatoes, chopped		

1.   Salt eggplant slices. Place under a weighted tray for ½ hour. Rinse and drain.

2.   Arrange eggplant on an oiled sheet, sprinkle with half the oil and brown under broiler.

3.   Heat remaining oil, add garlic and cook briefly (do not brown). Add tomatoes, basil, salt and red and black peppers to taste. Simmer 15 minutes.

4.   Cut eggplant slices into 2-inch pieces and toss with hot, cooked pasta. Sauce lightly and garnish with parsley.

NOTE: This dish is light and meatless, without all the oil usually associated with eggplant. Serve as a main course or a side dish.

Linguine con Pesto
Linguine with Basil and Garlic
Serves 4 to 6

1	pound linguine
1	recipe for Pesto (page 119), at room temperature

Freshly grated Parmigiano
Toasted pine nuts

1.   Cook the linguine in salted boiling water until it is al dente. Drain the pasta leaving it slightly wet. Transfer it to a saucepan and add the Pesto. Toss quickly over very low heat, then transfer the linguine to a warm serving bowl and sprinkle it with the grated Parmigiano and pine nuts.

NOTE: An alternate method is to heat the Pesto slightly first. Drain the cooked linguine and transfer it to a warm serving bowl. Add the Pesto to the linguine and toss rapidly to distribute the Pesto evenly over the linguine. Sprinkle with the Parmigiano and toasted pine nuts. Serve immediately.

Fettuccine all' Andrea
Fettuccine with Zucchini and Mushrooms in Cream Sauce
Serves 4 to 6

1   pound fettuccine
6   tablespoons butter
1½   cups thinly sliced mushrooms
2   small zucchini, cut into
     ⅛-inch julienne (may use
     food processor)

1   large carrot, peeled and cut
     to match the zucchini
1½   cups heavy cream
     Salt and freshly ground
     black pepper
½   cup freshly grated
     Parmigiano

1.   Melt 3 tablespoons of the butter in a skillet. Add the mushrooms, carrots and zucchini and cook until tender.
2.   Cook the fettuccine in salted boiling water until it is al dente.
3.   In a large skillet, heat the cream over low heat. Add the butter, vegetables, salt and pepper. Heat slowly.
4.   Drain the pasta and add it to the cream mixture in the pan. Add the Parmigiano and toss quickly to coat the pasta.
5.   Serve immediately with additional Parmigiano and black pepper.

Fettuccine con Pesto e Panna
Fettuccine with Pesto and Cream
Serves 4 to 6

1 pound fettuccine	Salt and freshly ground
1 recipe for Pesto (page 119)	black pepper
1½ cups heavy cream	Freshly grated Parmigiano
	Toasted pine nut

1.   Cook the fettuccine in salted boiling water until it is al dente. While the fettuccine is cooking, prepare the sauce. Heat the Pesto in a large skillet and add the cream, salt and pepper (see Note). Whisk over high heat until smooth and creamy.

2.   Drain the fettuccine and transfer it to a warm serving bowl. Pour the sauce over the fettuccine and toss well. Sprinkle with the Parmigiano and pine nuts and serve immediately.

NOTE: Freshly grated nutmeg may also be added to the sauce.

Fettuccini alla Romana
Fettuccine with Cream and Parmigiano
Serves 4 to 6

1	pound fettuccine
1½	cups heavy cream
16	tablespoons sweet butter
	Scant pinch of freshly grated nutmeg

Salt and freshly ground black pepper

⅔ cup freshly grated Parmigiano

1. Cook the fettuccine in salted boiling water until it is al dente.
2. While the fettuccine is cooking, heat the cream, butter, nutmeg, salt and pepper over very low heat. Whisk constantly for 1 minute.
3. Drain the noodles and add them to the sauce in the pan. Sprinkle with the Parmigiano and toss quickly to coat all the noodles.
5. Serve immediately with additional grated Parmigiano and black pepper.

Fettuccine con Gorgonzola
Fettuccine with Gorgonzola
Serves 4 to 6

1 pound fettuccine	4 ounces Gorgonzola (the soft variety) broken into small pieces
½ cup clarified butter (page 309)	
4 garlic cloves, finely chopped	
¼ cup dry white wine	1 cup light cream
½ cup chicken stock (page 65)	2 ounces freshly grated Parmigiano
1 cup chopped, peeled and seeded tomatoes	Salt and freshly ground black pepper
8 fresh basil leaves, stems removed	¼ cup pine nuts, toasted

1.   Cook the fettuccine in boiling salted water until it is al dente.

2.   While it is cooking, prepare the sauce. Heat the butter in a very large skillet. Add the garlic and sauté for 30 seconds. Raise the heat, add the white wine and let it reduce to about 3 tablespoons. Add the stock and let reduce for 1 to 2 minutes. Add the tomatoes, basil and Gorgonzola. Lower the heat and stir rapidly to melt the cheese. Add the cream, salt and pepper. Raise the heat and let the sauce reduce for 1 minute more. Lower heat.

3.   Drain the fettuccine and add it to the sauce in the pan. Toss well to coat all the noodles with the sauce, then remove from the heat. Add half of the grated cheese and all but 2 tablespoons of the pine nuts and toss again.

4.   Serve immediately with the extra grated Parmigiano and pine nuts sprinkled on top.

NOTE: For a different but equally delicious dish, omit the tomatoes and basil.

Fettuccine con Formaggio e Proscuitto
Fettuccine with Cheese and Prosciutto
Serves 4 to 6

1	pound fettuccine	6	slices prosciutto, trimmed
¼	cup clarified butter (page 309)		of fat, cut into ¼-inch
2	garlic cloves, finely chopped		pieces
¼	cup dry white wine		Salt and freshly ground
½	cup chicken stock (page 65)		black pepper
2	ounces fontina, grated	2	ounces freshly grated
2	ounces ricotta cup light cream		Parmigiano

1.   Cook the fettuccine in boiling salted water until it is al dente.

2.   While the fettuccine is cooking, prepare the sauce. Heat the butter in a large skillet. Add the garlic and sauté for 30 seconds (do not burn it). Raise the heat and add the wine. Let the wine reduce to about 3 tablespoons. Add the stock and let it reduce again for 1 to 2 minutes. Lower the heat, add the cheeses and stir until they are melted. Add the cream, prosciutto, salt and pepper. Let reduce for 1 minute. Lower the heat.

3.   Drain the fettuccine and add it to the sauce in the pan. Toss well to coat all the noodles. Sprinkle with the grated Parmigiano and toss again. Serve immediately.

Fettuccine con Salmone e Tartufi
Fettuccine with Salmon and Truffles
Serves 4

1	cup fish stock (page 67)	8	fresh basil leaves, stems
1	cup shrimp shells, if available		removed
1	pound fettuccine	½	pound smoked salmon, cut
2	tablespoons brandy		into thin strips
2	bay leaves	1	large egg yolk
1	cup heavy cream		Salt and freshly ground
1	tablespoon white or black		white pepper
	truffles, thinly sliced or shaved		

1.   Combine the stock and shrimp shells in a saucepan and bring to a boil. Lower the heat and simmer for 15 minutes. Strain out the shells and return the stock to the pan.

2.   Cook the fettuccine in boiling salted water until it is al dente.

3.   While the fettuccine is cooking, finish the sauce. Add the brandy, bay leaves, truffles (reserve a couple for garnish) and cream to the stock. Let the sauce reduce for 2 minutes. Add 12 strips of the salmon and 6 of the basil leaves. Then whisk in the egg yolk and season with salt and pepper.

4.   Drain the fettuccine and transfer it to a warm serving bowl. Pour the sauce over the fettuccine and toss well. Garnish with the extra salmon, basil and truffles. Serve immediately.

Fettucini with Squid
Fettucini con Calamari
Serves 6

1   pound fetttucini, cooked al dente

1   pound squid, cleaned and cut into ½-inch strips

3   tablespoons olive oil

3   cloves garlic, minced

¾   cup dry white wine

¼   cup dry red wine

1   teaspoon oregano

2   tablespoons chopped, fresh basil

¼   teaspoon dried rosemary

4   cups stemmed, chopped Swiss chard

1.   Quickly sauté squid and garlic in oil for 2 minutes then remove.

2.   Add wines and herbs to pan and cook on high for 2 minutes. Add chard and cook another 4 minutes.

3.   Return squid to pan and heat 1 minute. Toss with hot pasta.

Penne all' Arrabbiata
Angry Penne
Serves 4 To 6

5	tablespoons olive oil		Pinch of hot red pepper
2	garlic cloves, finely chopped or pressed		flakes
			Salt
2	ounces pancetta	1	pound penne
1½	cups Italian plum tomatoes, passed through a sieve	2	ounces Pecorino Romano, or Parmigiano, freshly grated
2	parsley sprigs		

1.   Heat the oil in a non-stick saucepan. Add the garlic and sauté over low heat for 1 minute. Raise the heat slightly, add the pancetta and brown on both sides. Add the tomatoes, parsley, hot pepper flakes and salt. Cover and cook over moderate heat for 20 minutes. Discard the meat and parsley.

2.   In the meantime, cook the penne in salted boiling water until it is al dente.

3.   Drain the penne and add it to the sauce in the pan. Add the grated Pecorino and cook for 2 minutes over high heat, tossing the penne to coat it with the sauce. Serve immediately with the grated Parmigiano.

Penne con Crema, Formaggio e Pomodore
Penne with Cream, Cheese and Tomato
Serves 4 to 6

1	pound penne, cooked for 5 minutes only	½	cup grated Romano cheese
2	cups heavy cream	4	tablespoons Gorganzola cheese, crumbled
1	cup Italian plum tomatoes, chopped	2	tablespoons ricotta cheese
1	tablespoon tomato paste	10	basil leaves, chopped
		4	tablespoons butter

1.   In a large bowl, combine all ingredients except butter. Toss to coat penne evenly.

2.   Arrange on an ovenproof platter and dot with butter. Bake in a pre-heated 375-degree oven until brown on top, about 15 minutes.

Penne con Asparagi e Funghi
Penne with Asparagus and Mushrooms
Serves 6

4	tablespoons olive oil	4	cups Marinara Sauce
1	pound asparagus, cut in		(page 116)
	1-inch pieces	1	pound penne, cooked al dente
2	cups sliced mushrooms		Parsley or fresh basil

1.   Sauté asparagus in 2 tablespoons of the oil over medium-high heat, 4 to 5 minutes. Season with salt and pepper and set aside.

2.   Add another 2 tablespoons oil to pan and briefly sauté the mushrooms. Do not over-cook.

3.   Add asparagus and mushrooms to Marinara Sauce and cook for 5 minutes. Toss with hot, cooked penne. Garnish with basil or parsley.

Maruzzelle con Funghi e Radicchio
Pasta Shells with Mushrooms and Radicchio
Serves 4 to 6

1	pound maruzzelle, cooked for 5 minutes only	2	cups radicchio, shredded
		2	cups half and half cream
8	ounces white mushrooms, sliced	1	cup heavy cream
		2	cups Parmigiano, grated
5	dried mushrooms (boletus or porcini), soaked and sliced	½	cup fontina cheese, grated
		½	cup ricotta cheese
1	stick butter	8	leaves fresh sage, minced

1.   Sauté mushrooms in 6 tablespoons butter 4 to 5 minutes. Reserve remaining 2 tablespoons butter.

2.   Combine all ingredients except butter and mix well. Add the cooked pasta and season with salt and pepper.

3.   Arrange on an oven-proof platter, dot with remainning butter and bake in a preheated 450-degree oven until the top is lightly browned, about 10 minutes. Garnish with fresh sage.

Pasta con Funghi e Noci
Pasta with Mushrooms and Nuts
Serves 4 to 6

1	pound any type thin pasta, cooked al dente	¾	cup dry Marsala or dry sherry
4	tablespoons canola or olive oil	2	cups peeled, seeded and chopped tomatoes
4	shallots, finely chopped	½	cup fresh basil, chopped
1	pound fresh mushrooms, sliced		Salt and pepper to taste
¾	ounce dried porcini mushrooms, soaked in water	¼	cup slivered almonds
		¼	cup pine nuts

1. Sauté shallots in 3 tablespoons of oil until wilted. Add mushrooms and cook for 3 minutes. Add wine, tomatoes and basil and simmer, uncovered, for about 15 minutes.
2. Brown nuts in 1 tablespoon oil. Toss hot pasta in sauce and top with nuts.

Brocoletti di Rabe con Farfalle
Broccoli Rabe with Farfalle
Serves 4

1	pound farfalle, cooked al dente	1½	pounds broccoli rabe, rinsed and chopped
5	tablespoons olive oil		Juice of ½ lemon
4	cloves garlic, finely chopped		Salt and black pepper to taste
8	anchovy fillets, finely chopped		

1.   Heat oil in a large pan. Add garlic and anchovies and cook over high heat until garlic begins to brown.

2.   Add chopped greens and toss until greens begin to wilt (2 to 3 minutes). Season with lemon juice, salt and freshly ground pepper. Toss with hot, cooked pasta.

Tortellini con Panna
Tortellini with Cream
Serves 4

60	tortellini	2	large egg yolks
4	tablespoons butter	6	tablespoons freshly grated
2	tablespoons brandy		Parmigiano
1½	cups heavy cream		Salt and freshly ground
½	teaspoon freshly grated		white pepper
	nutmeg		

1.   Cook the tortellini in salted boiling water until al dente.

2.   While the tortellini is cooking, prepare the sauce. Melt the butter in a heavy skillet. Raise the heat, add the brandy and let it burn off. Add the cream and nutmeg and reduce for 1 minute.

3.   Drain the tortellini and transfer it to a warm serving bowl.

4.   Whisk the egg yolks and 4 tablespoons of the grated Parmigiano into the sauce. Season with salt and pepper. Pour the sauce over the tortellini, sprinkle with the remaining Parmigiano and serve immediately.

Lasagne al Forno
Lasagne with Ragù and Cheese
Serves 6

1	tablespoon olive oil
	Salt
13	strips curly edged lasagne noodles
4	cups Ragù (page 117)
1	pound ground beef sautéed or made into marble-size meatballs. (Use the Polpette recipe, page 62)
¾	pound Italian sweet sausages, cooked and thinly sliced
1½	pounds whole milk ricotta, drained of excess liquid
½	pound whole milk mozzarella, finely chopped
5	tablespoons freshly grated Parmigiano
4	hard-boiled large eggs, chopped
1	cup Balsamella (page 267)
	Freshly ground black pepper

1.   Cook the lasagne until al dente. Drain and cool in cold water. Lay the noodles in a single layer on a cloth towel.

2.   Cover the bottom of a 9- by 13- by 2-inch baking pan with a thin layer of the Ragù. Lay 5 strips of noodles along the width of the pan. Spread half of all the remaining ingredients in layers over the noodles. Pour a generous amount of the Ragù and ½ cup of the Balsamella over the ingredients (do not flood with sauce).

3.   Lay 3 strips of noodles lengthwise over the first layer. Spread the remaining half of the ingredients in layers over the noodles. Cover with Ragù and the remaining Balsamella.

4.   Layer the remaining noodles along the width of the pan. Pour the remaining Ragù over the noodles and sprinkle with the Parmigiano.

5.   Cover the pan with foil and bake for 25 minutes at 375 degrees. Remove foil and bake for 10 minutes more. Let stand for 5 minutes before serving.

Lasagne Verdi
Spinach Lasagne with Four Cheeses
Serves 6

1	tablespoon olive oil	6	hard-boiled large eggs, chopped
	Salt		
13	strips curly edged spinach lasagne	¾	cup fresh grated Parmigiano
		¾	cup fresh grated Pecorino Romano
3	tablespoons butter, melted		
2½	pounds whole milk ricotta, drained of excess liquid	1½	cups Balsamella (page 267)
		4	large eggs, beaten
½	pound whole milk mozzarella, finely chopped		Freshly ground black pepper

1.   Bring a large pot of water to a boil. Add the oil and a generous amount of salt. Cook the lasagne until they are al dente. Drain and cool in cold water, then pat them dry with paper towels. Lay the noodles in a single layer on a cloth towel, but do not overlap them.

2.   Preheat the oven to 375 degrees.

3.   Brush the bottom of a 9- by 13- by 2-inch baking pan with 1½ tablespoons of the butter. Arrange the layers of noodles as in the recipe for Lasagne al Forno. Spread half of the remaining ingredients on the 2 layers. (Reserve some Parmigiano.) Brush the final layer with the remaining butter and sprinkle with the grated Parmigiano.

3.   Cover the pan with aluminum foil and bake for 25 minutes. Remove the foil and continue baking for 5 minutes. Let stand for 5 minutes before serving. If desired, spread with extra Balsamella before serving.

Lasagne alla Veneziana
Spinach Lasagne Layered with Broccoli, Zucchini, Veal and Chicken
Serves 6

1	tablespoon olive oil Salt		1	cup freshly grated Pecorino Romano
13	strips curly edged spinach lasagne		½	pound cooked chicken, chopped
1½	tablespoons melted butter		½	pound ground veal, sautéed
1½	pounds whole milk ricotta, drained of excess liquid		½	cup Balsamella (page 267)
2	cups chopped broccoli flowerets		1½	cups Espagnole Sauce (page 271)
1½	cups chopped zucchini			Freshly ground black pepper
1	cup thinly sliced fresh mushrooms			

1. Bring a large pot of water to a boil. Add the olive oil and a generous amount of salt. Cook the lasagne until they are al dente. Drain and cool in cold water, then pat them dry with paper towels. Lay the noodles in a single layer on a cloth towel, but do not overlap them.

2. Preheat the oven to 375 degrees.

3. Brush the bottom of a 9- by 13- by 2-inch baking pan with the melted butter. Arrange the noodles as in the recipe for Lasagne al Forno. Spread half of all the ingredients on the 2 layers. Reserve ½ cup of the Espagnole Sauce.

4. Pour the remaining Espagnole Sauce over the top of the lasagne. Cover with aluminum foil and bake for 25 minutes. Remove the foil and bake 5 minutes more. Let stand for 5 minutes before serving.

5. Serve with additional Balsamella and Espagnole sauces if desired.

Crespelle
Crêpes
Makes 18 Crespelle

5	large eggs	½	teaspoon salt
1½	cups milk	½	cup vegetable oil
1	cup water		
2	cups all purpose flower		

1.   In a mixing bowl, beat together the eggs, milk, water and salt with a wire whisk. Add the flour a little at a time, beat until thoroughly blended. Cover the batter and refrigerate for 2 hours.

2.   Heat an 8-inch crêpe pan. Rub the bottom of the pan with a paper towel dipped in vegetable oil.

3.   Pour ¼ cup of the batter into the pan. Tilt the pan immediately so that the batter spreads over the entire bottom of the pan. Cook the crespelle quickly on one side only. Remove the crespelle from the pan by turning the pan over onto a plate. Stack the crespelle and keep covered until ready to use.

Note: Using water instead of all milk makes these crepes extra tender and delicate.

Crespelle Verdi
Spinach Crepes
Makes 18 Crespelle

2   cups fresh spinach, leaves only   1   recipe for crespelle batter
Pinch salt   (page 107)

1.   Carefully wash the spinach and leave it wet. Lightly steam the spinach in its own water, adding a pinch of salt.
2.   When the spinach has wilted, drain it and squeeze out all the excess liquid, then chop it finely.
3.   Mix the spinach together with 1 cup of the batter. Then mix this into the remaining batter.
4.   Cook as for regular crespelle.

Manicotti
Stuffed Crepes with Black Olives and Prosciutto
Serves 6

2	pounds whole milk ricotta		Salt and freshly ground
1	large egg		black pepper
1	cup freshly grated Parmigiano	12	thin slices prosciutto,
¼	cup finely chopped walnuts		trimmed of excess fat
¼	cup blanched slivered almonds	12	crespelle (page 107)
¼	cup finely chopped black olives	12	thin slices whole milk
¼	cup finely chopped fresh		mozzarella
	parsley	2	cups Ragù (page 117)
1	tablespoon dried basil or		
	finely chopped fresh basil		

1.   Preheat the oven to 450 degrees.

2.   In a large mixing bowl combine the ricotta, eggs, ½ cup of the Parmigiano, walnuts, almonds, olives, parsley, basil, salt and pepper. Mix well.

3.   Lay the crespelle, browned side up, on work surface.

4.   Place 1 slice of prosciutto on each crespelle. Top with a large scoop of the ricotta mixture (about ¼ cup). Fold half of the crespella over the cheese, fold in the sides and then fold over the other half. The manicotti will be tubular shaped.

5.   Spread half of the sauce over the bottom of a large baking pan. Arrange the manicotti, seam side up, in the pan. Cover with the remaining sauce. Be careful not to drown the manicotti in sauce.

6.   Cover the pan with aluminum foil and bake for 15 minutes. Remove the foil, cover each roll with a slice of mozzarella and sprinkle all with the remaining Parmigiano. Return to the oven, uncovered, for 5 minutes, or until the cheese has melted. Serve immediately.

Manicotti Verdi
Stuffed Spinach Crepes with Chicken and Herbs
Serves 6

2	pounds whole milk ricotta	1	tablespoon chopped fresh basil
1	pound fresh spinach		
1	cup freshly grated Parmigiano	½	teaspoon dried marjoram
1	cup finely chopped fresh parsley		Salt and freshly ground black pepper
1	large egg	12	crespelle verdi (page 108)
2	cups cooked chicken, coarsely chopped (about 1 whole breast)	⅔	cup butter, melted
		12	thin slices whole milk mozzarella

1.   Preheat the oven to 450 degrees.

2.   Using a double thickness of cheesecloth, squeeze any excess liquid from the ricotta.

3.   Clean the spinach and leave it wet. Steam the spinach lightly in its own water with a little salt. Drain, squeeze out the excess water and chop the spinach finely.

4.   In a large mixing bowl, combine the ricotta, ½ cup of the Parmigiano, spinach, parsley, egg, chicken, basil, marjoram, salt and pepper. Mix well.

5.   Lay the crespelle, browned side up, on the work surface. Place a large scoop of the ricotta mixture (about ½ cup) onto each crespella. Fold half of the crespella over the cheese, fold in the sides and then fold over the other half.

6.   Brush a large baking pan with melted butter. Arrange the manicotti seam side up in the pan and brush with melted butter.

7.   Cover with aluminum foil and bake for 20 minutes. Remove the foil and top each roll with a slice of mozzarella and a sprinkle of grated Parmigiano. Return to the oven, uncovered, and bake for 5 minutes more, or until the cheese has melted. Serve immediately.

Cannelloni alla Genovese
Seafood Cannelloni
Serves 6

12	crespelle (page 107)	½	cup finely chopped fresh parsley leaves
2	pounds shrimp, shelled (Reserve the shells.)		Salt and freshly ground black pepper
1	pound haddock or flounder	3	cups fish stock (page 67)
1	cup steamed mussels, shelled	3	bay leaves
1	cup bay scallops	½	cup dry white wine
¼	cup white wine	1	cup heavy cream
½	fresh lemon	1	teaspoon tomato paste
6	large egg yolks	¼	teaspoon freshly grated nutmeg
2	cups ricotta		Salt and freshly ground white pepper
1	cup finely chopped mozzarella		
½	cup dry sherry		
⅛	teaspoon cayenne pepper		
½	teaspoon freshly grated nutmeg		

1.   Preheat the oven to 450 degrees.

2.   Poach the shrimp, scallops and haddock in water with the white wine and lemon. Drain and shock in ice water. Drain again. Chop the shrimp, fish and mussels. Combine all the seafood in a large bowl.

3.   Add the egg yolks, ricotta, mozzarella, sherry, cayenne, nutmeg, parsley, salt and black pepper. Mix well.

4.   Lay the crespelle, brown side up, on a work surface. Place a large scoop of the seafood mixture on each. Roll one end first, then the sides up over the filling. Fold over the remaining half. The cannelloni will be tubular shaped. Place them in a buttered baking pan. Cover with aluminum foil and bake for 15 to 20 minutes.

5.   While the cannelloni is baking, prepare the sauce. Combine the stock, reserved shrimp shells, bay leaves and wine in a saucepan. Bring to a boil and simmer for 20 minutes. Strain the shells and bay leaves from the stock, and return it to the pan. Add the cream and reduce by half. Dissolve the tomato paste in ½ cup of the sauce and add this to the pan. Season with nutmeg, salt and white pepper.

6.   Cover the bottom of the serving plate with a little sauce. Arrange the cannelloni on top and pour a little more of the sauce over the cannelloni. Serve immediately.

Cannelloni Verdi
Stuffed Spinach Crepes with Veal, Pork and Chicken
Serves 6

½	cup butter, melted	1½	tablespoons dried basil or chopped fresh basil leaves
2	tablespoons dry sherry		
1	pound ground veal	1½	teaspoons pressed garlic
	Salt and freshly ground black pepper	½	teaspoon dried thyme
½	pound ground pork	½	cup freshly grated Parmigiano
½	pound spinach		
1	cup coarsely chopped cooked chicken (about ½ breast)	½	cup finely chopped fresh parsley
		12	crespelle verdi (page 108)
1	pound whole milk ricotta, drained of excess liquid	1	cup Balsamella (page 267)
1	large egg	½	cup Espagnole Sauce (page 271)

1.   Preheat the oven to 450 degrees.

2.   Heat a little of the butter in a frying pan and sauté the veal with the sherry until it is just done. Season with salt and pepper. Remove the veal

to a large mixing bowl.

3.   In the same pan, heat more of the butter and sauté the pork until it is just done. Season with salt and pepper. Add the pork to the veal.

4.   Clean the spinach and leave it wet. Steam it lightly with its own water and a little salt. Drain, squeeze out the excess water and chop the spinach finely. Add it to the cooked meats.

5.   Add all the remaining ingredients, except the crespelle, Balsamella and Espagnole Sauce to the meat and spinach. Mix thoroughly. Season with salt and pepper.

6.   Lay the crespelle, browned side up, on the work surface.

7.   Place a large scoop of the mixture (about ½ cup) on each crespella. Fold as for Cannelloni alla Genovese.

8.   Brush a large baking pan with melted butter. Arrange the cannelloni, seam side up, in the pan. Pour the Balsamella over the cannelloni and pour the Espagnole sauce over the Balsamella.

9.   Cover with aluminum foil and bake for 20 minutes.

Serve immediately.

Cannelloni
Stuffed Crepes with Chicken Livers and Mushrooms
Serves 6

¼　cup butter, melted
1　pound ground veal
½　teaspoon dried thyme
1　tablespoon dried basil
2　tablespoons dry white wine
　　Salt and freshly ground black pepper
　　Juice of ½ lemon
½　pound ground beef
1　pound chicken livers, finely chopped
½　cup coarsely chopped cooked chicken (about ¼ breast)

½　cup finely chopped fresh mushrooms
1　pound whole milk ricotta, drained of excess liquid
1　large egg
½　cup freshly grated Parmigiano
½　cup finely chopped fresh parsley leaves
12　crespelle (page 107)
3　cups Ragù (page 117)

1.　Heat a little of the butter in a frying pan and sauté the veal with the thyme, basil and wine. Add the lemon juice to the veal once it is cooked. Season with salt and pepper. Remove the veal to a large mixing bowl.

2.　Preheat the oven to 450 degrees.

3.　In the same frying pan, heat a little more butter and sauté the beef until it is just done. Season with salt and pepper.

4.　Add the beef and all the remaining ingredients, except the crespelle and Ragù, to the veal, and mix thoroughly. Season with salt and pepper.

5.　Lay the crespella, browned side up, on the work surface. Place a large scoop of the veal mixture (about ½ cup) on each crespella. Roll as for Cannelloni alla Genovese.

6.　Spread half of the Ragù sauce over the bottom of a large baking pan. Arrange the cannelloni, seam side up, in the pan. Cover with the remaining sauce. Be careful not to drown the cannelloni in sauce. Cover with aluminum foil and bake for 25 minutes. Serve immediately with extra grated Parmigiano.

Salsa di Pomodoro Semplice
Simple Tomato Sauce
Makes enough for 1 pound of pasta

This is a tomato sauce that is very easy to make.

2	tablespoons olive oil	1	pound Italian plum
1	ounce pancetta, cut into thin		tomatoes, peeled and seeded
	strips	6	fresh basil leaves, chopped
2	garlic cloves, sliced thin	2	parsley sprigs, leaves only
	A tiny piece of dried red		Salt
	pepper or a pinch of hot red		
	pepper flakes		

1.   Heat the olive oil in a saucepan. Add the pancetta and garlic, lower the heat and lightly brown both. Remove them from the pan and discard.
2.   Add the remaining ingredients and simmer for 30 minutes to 1 hour. Mash the tomatoes with a fork as they cook.

Note: For a thicker sauce, add a teaspoon of tomato paste.

Salsa Marinara
Tomato and Vegetable Sauce
Makes 1 quart

3	tablespoons olive oil		1	teaspoon dried oregano
2	garlic cloves, chopped finely		1	tablespoon dried basil, or
1	onion, chopped			fresh basil leaves
½	celery stalk, sliced on an		½	sweet green pepper, chopped
	angle		10	pitted black olives, chopped
1	35-ounce can imported			Pinch of hot red pepper
	Italian tomatoes, seeded			flakes
	and coarsely chopped		1	teaspoon salt
½	cup dry white wine		½	teaspoon freshly ground
1	tablespoon red wine vinegar			black pepper
1	bay leaf		2	tablespoons finely chopped
½	teaspoon dried rosemary or			fresh parsley leaves
	chopped fresh rosemary leaves			

1.   Heat the oil in a saucepan. Add the garlic, onions and celery, and sauté until the onion and garlic are lightly browned.
2.   Add all the other ingredients and bring to a boil. Lower the heat and simmer for 25 minutes.
3.   Use immediately or cool completely and refrigerate.

Ragù
Meat Sauce
Makes 3½ quarts

¼   cup olive oil
1½ pounds each veal and beef
    bones
½   pound salt pork
5   garlic cloves, finely chopped
2   carrots, finely chopped
4   onions, finely chopped
2   celery stalks, finely chopped
2   28-ounce cans Italian plum
    tomatoes, seeded and
    coarsely chopped

1   28-ounce can tomato puree
2   6-ounce cans tomato paste
1   cup dry red wine
1   cup water
2   tablespoons dried basil
2   bay leaves
½   teaspoon hot red pepper
    flakes
    Salt and freshly ground
    black pepper

1.   Heat the oil in a large heavy saucepan. Add the bones and the salt pork and cook for 20 minutes, stirring occasionally. Remove bones and salt pork and discard.
2.   Add the garlic to the pan and brown lightly, then add the onions, carrots and celery and sauté until the vegetables are tender.
3.   Add all the remaining ingredients and bring to a boil. Lower the heat and simmer for 2 hours, stirring occasionally.
4.   Refrigerate in airtight containers or freeze in small amounts.

Ragù II
Meat Sauce
Makes enough for 1 pound of pasta

¼   cup olive oil
10   ounces ground pork
3   ounces pancetta, ground
1   small onion, finely chopped
1   small carrot, peeled and
     finely chopped
1   celery stalk, finely chopped

1   garlic clove, finely chopped
     (optional)
1   cup meat broth (page 63)
1   heaping teaspoon tomato
     paste
     Salt and freshly ground
     black pepper

1.   Heat the oil in a saucepan or large skillet. Add the ground pork, pancetta, onion, carrot, celery and garlic, and brown over high heat.
2.   Add the broth and tomato paste and stir well over high heat. Season with salt and pepper, then cover the contents of the pan with cold water and bring to a boil. Lower the heat and simmer for 30 to 45 minutes.

NOTE: This sauce can be made extra special by adding a few shavings of fresh truffles and some grated Parmigiano just before serving.

Pesto
Basil and Garlic Sauce
Makes enough for 1 pound of spaghetti

2	cups fresh basil leaves without stems	2	tablespoons pine nuts (walnuts may be substituted)
¾	cup extra virgin olive oil	⅔	cup freshly grated Parmigiano
5	garlic cloves, peeled		Salt and freshly ground black pepper

1.   Combine all the ingredients in an electric blender or food processor. Blend on the highest speed until smooth.

2.   If the Pesto is not to be used immediately, place it in a container and cover it with ½ inch of olive oil. Seal tightly. The Pesto may also be frozen in the same manner.

Salsa di Pepperoni
Pepper Sauce
Serves 6

1	cup defatted chicken broth	1	medium red onion, diced
8	large red bell peppers, skinned	2	cloves garlic, minced
10	large tomatoes, skinned and seeded	1	cup sweet sherry
			Salt and pepper to taste

1.   Blacken peppers over an open flame. Peel under cold water. Cut into cubes.

2.   Place tomatoes in boiling water for 2 minutes. Remove and peel. Cut in half, squeeze out seeds, dice.

3.   Heat broth, add onions and garlic. When onions are translucent add peppers and tomatoes. Simmer for 15 minutes, add sherry, salt and pepper.

4.   Cook over medium heat for 10 minutes. Remove from heat and purée.

NOTE: If desired, add a non-dairy cream, or skim milk for a lighter color.

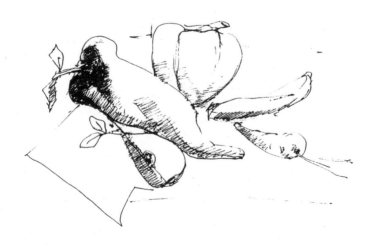

Polenta
Cornmeal
Serves 4

6   cups veal, chicken or beef   ½   pound stone-ground yellow
     stock, (pages 64, 45, and 63)   cornmeal
     or water or milk

1.   Bring the stock to a boil in a heavy saucepan. The liquid you use will depend on which flavor you desire; it should complement the food it is to accompany.
2.   Pour the cornmeal very slowly into the boiling liquid while stirring constantly with a wooden spoon. Lower the heat and cook the polenta for about 20 to 40 minutes, stirring constantly throughout the cooking period.
3.   Season with salt and pepper, then stir in the butter.
4.   Remove from the heat and transfer the polenta to a warm serving plate. Allow it to sit for 5 to 10 minutes. Slice or spoon it into portions and serve it with any very flavorful food. It will act as a perfect foil to strongly flavored dishes such as grilled or braised meats and fowl.
5.   Another option is to spread the polenta on a flat baking sheet. Allow the polenta to set until very firm. Slice it into rectangles and grill it. This, again, would be used as an accompaniment for strongly flavored or spicy foods.
6.   If milk is used to make the polenta, it makes an excellent first course. It may be seasoned with fresh herbs and should be served with freshly grated Parmigiano. .

Polenta al Quattro Formaggi
Polenta with Four Cheeses
Serves 4

6   cups chicken stock (page 65)
½   pound stone-ground yellow
      cornmeal
1   ounce fontina, cut into small
      cubes
1   ounce fresh mozzarella, cut
      into small cubes

1   ounce Gorgonzola
      (the soft variety)
⅛   cup freshly grated
      Parmigiano
      Salt and freshly ground
      black pepper
2   tablespoons butter, at room
      temperature

1.   Bring the chicken stock to a boil in a heavy saucepan. (If stock is not available, water may be substituted with excellent results.)

2.   Pour the cornmeal very slowly into the boiling stock while stirring constantly with a wooden spoon. Lower the heat and cook the polenta for 30 minutes, stirring constantly throughout the cooking period.

3.   Add the cheeses to the polenta and continue to stir until melted. Season with salt and pepper, then stir in the butter.

4.   Remove from the heat and transfer the polenta to a warm serving plate. Serve immediately with extra grated Parmigiano. The polenta may be used as a first or main course.

Polenta con Funghi alla Griglia
Polenta with Grilled Mushrooms

Prepare the polenta of your choice. Then clean any assortment of fresh, wild mushrooms. Coat them with a mixture of extra virgin olive oil, salt, freshly ground black pepper, chopped fresh rosemary leaves and minced garlic. Grill, broil or braise the mushrooms. A grill creates the best flavor. Serve the mushrooms over the polenta.

Risotto alla Milanese
Rice with Saffron and Parmigiano
Serves 4

5	tablespoons sweet butter, at room temperature		Pinch of saffron threads
⅓	cup finely chopped onion		Salt and freshly ground black pepper
1	cup Arborio rice	½	cup freshly grated Parmigiano
¼	cup dry white wine		
3½ to 4 cups hot chicken stock (page 65)			

1.   Melt 4 tablespoons of the butter in a heavy saucepan or casserole. Add the onion and sauté until it is translucent. Add the rice and sauté over low heat for 4 to 5 minutes, stirring constantly.

2.   Add the wine and simmer until it has reduced completely. Add ¼ cup of the stock and stir gently until all the stock has been absorbed. Continue to add the stock ¼ cup at a time, stirring constantly each time, until all the liquid has been absorbed. Once the first cup of stock has been used, add the saffron to the remaining stock. Cook the rice until it is al dente (the

rice should be creamy, not dry). This will take 15 to 20 minutes.

3.   When the rice is al dente, season it with salt and pepper and remove it from the heat. Stir in the remaining tablespoon of butter and the grated Parmigiano. Serve immediately with additional grated Parmigiano.

Risotto alla Milanese con Funghi
Rice Milanese
Serves 6

1	ounce dried mushrooms (porcini or boletus)	¼	cup white wine
		4	cups chicken stock
5	tablespoons olive oil		pinch of saffron threads
⅓	cup finely chopped onion	¼	cup grated Parmigiano
1	cup rice (Arborio or Carolina)		Salt and pepper

1.   Soak the mushrooms in tepid water for 15 minutes.

2.   In a heavy pan, sauté onion in oil until limp. Lower heat, add rice, stirring constantly. Add wine, stirring until absorbed.

3.   Crumble saffron into stock and add stock, ¼ cup at a time, while continuing to stir. Cook until al dente, 15 to 20 minutes.

4.   Add mushrooms and heat through. Turn off heat and add Parmigiano and salt and pepper to taste.

NOTE: This dish is traditionally prepared with butter.

Risotto alla Piemontese
Risotto Piedmontese
Serves 4

3	tablespoons olive oil	6	cups spinach, stemmed and chopped
1	medium red onion, finely chopped	⅓	cup dry white wine
½	cup finely chopped carrot	2	cups chicken broth, heated to boiling
½	cup finely chopped celery hearts		Salt and pepper to taste
1	cup Arborio rice		Parsley for garnish

1.   In a deep pan sauté onion in oil until wilted. Add carrots and celery and cook for 10 minutes. Add rice and stir to coat well. Cook over low heat for 10 minutes.

2.   Add half of broth, cook 10 minutes, then add remaining broth and cook another 10 minutes.

3.   Add spinach, wine, salt and pepper and heat through. If rice is too firm add a little more broth or wine and cook a few more minutes. Garnish with parsley.

Risotto con Melanzane e Funghi
Rice with Eggplant and Mushrooms

2	cups Arborio rice	3	cups dry white wine
2	medium onions, chopped fine	2	tablespoons butter
3	cups cubed eggplant, with peel	4	tablespoons olive oil
1	pound mushrooms, caps sliced. stems minced	1	cup peeled and seeded tomatoes (fresh or canned Italian plum)
½	cup dry porcini, soaked in warm water	1	clove garlic, minced
¼	pound pancetta, chopped		salt and pepper
2	cups beef or chicken stock		

1.   In a deep pot sauté the onions in the butter. When onions wilt add garlic and tomatoes. Cook for 5 minutes. Add rice, stirring to coat thoroughly. Add the heated stock, a little at a time, stirring frequently.

2.   While rice is cooking heat oil in a skillet. When hot, add eggplant that has been salted, drained and patted dry. When eggplant starts to brown, add mushrooms. Chop the porcini and add to fresh mushrooms.

3.   Add the porcini soaking water. Cook quickly, stirring occasionally for 3 minutes. Add salt and pepper.

4.   When rice has absorbed the stock add the eggplant and mushrooms. Heat wine and add slowly. Rice should cook for 20 to 25 minutes. It should be tender but not soft.

Risotto con Funghi
Rice with Mushrooms and Parmigiano
Serves 4

1	ounce dried porcini mushrooms	3	fresh sage leaves, finely chopped
2	cups tepid water	¼	cup dry white wine
4	tablespoons clarified butter (page 309)	3	cups, approximately, hot veal stock (page 65) (Chicken stock may be used, though the flavor will be milder.) Salt and freshly ground black pepper
2	tablespoons finely chopped shallots		
2	teaspoons finely chopped garlic		
1	cup Arborio rice	1	tablespoon butter, at room temperature
¾	cup thinly sliced fresh mushrooms	½	cup freshly grated Parmigiano
¾	teaspoon dried thyme		
2	teaspoons finely chopped fresh rosemary leaves		

1.   Cover the porcini mushrooms with the tepid water. Weight them down with a plate, if necessary, to keep all the mushrooms submerged. Soak for 1 hour, then remove the mushrooms from the water and rinse them very well to remove all sand and dirt. Strain the soaking liquid through several layers of paper towels and reserve the liquid.

2.   Heat the clarified butter in a heavy saucepan. Add the shallots and garlic and sauté over low heat for 1 minute. Add the rice and sauté for 2 minutes, stirring the rice to coat it with the butter. Add the fresh mushrooms and cook for 2 minutes more. Stir in the thyme, rosemary, sage and wine and let the wine reduce completely.

3.   Heat the stock with ½ cup of the soaking liquid from the porcini.

4.   Cut the porcini mushrooms into bite-size pieces. Add the porcini to the rice. Start adding the stock very slowly (¼ cup at a time). Stir gently until all the stock is absorbed. Continue this process until all the stock is used and the rice is al dente, about 15 to 20 minutes. If more stock is needed, use only hot stock.

5.   Remove the pan from the heat and season the rice with salt and pepper. Add the butter and Parmigiano and mix very well. Serve immediately with additional grated Parmigiano, if desired.

Risotto con Piselli e Prosciutto
Rice with Peas and Prosciutto
Serve 6

½   cup virgin olive oil
½   large onion, minced
6   thin slices of prosciutto, minced
2   cups Arborio rice
1   cup fresh peas, blanched

2   teaspoons tomato paste
6   cups (approximately) hot chicken stock
    Salt and freshly ground black pepper
¾   cup grated Parmigiano cheese

1.   Heat the oil in a heavy-bottomed saucepan. Add the onions and sauté until translucent. Add the prosciutto and stir. Add the rice and cook for one minutes, stirring. Add the peas and stir.

2.   Dilute the tomato paste in a little of the chicken stock and add to the pan. Stir gently over low heat until all the liquid has been absorbed. Add the remaining stock, ¼ cup at a time, stirring after each addition, until all the stock is absorbed. This will take 15 to 20 minutes.

3.   When rice is al dente, season with salt and pepper and stir in grated Parmigiano. Serve immediately.

Risotto con Frutti di Mare
Rice with Shrimp, Mussels and Squid
Serves 6

¼ cup olive oil

4 tablespoons butter, at room temperature

½ medium onion, finely chopped

1 small carrot, finely chopped

½ stalk celery, finely chopped

4 sprigs of fresh parsley, leaves only, finely chopped

1 small bayleaf

4 ounces shrimp, peeled and deveined

4 ounces squid, cleaned and sliced into thin circles

4 ounces mussels, steamed and removed from the shells

3½ cups Arborio rice

¼ cup Cognac

1 cup dry white wine

10 cups, approximately, hot fish stock (page 67)

2 tablespoons finely chopped fresh basil leaves

Salt and freshly ground black pepper

1.   Heat the olive oil and 2 tablespoons of the butter together in a heavy-bottomed saucepan. Add the onion, carrot, celery, and bayleaf. Stir and sauté the vegetables until they are tender.

2.   Add the shrimp and squid and sauté until they are opaque. (If the shrimp are large, slice them in half through the back before sautéing.) Remove the shrimp and squid from the pan and set them aside with the cooked mussels.

3.   Add the rice to the pan and sauté for about 4 minutes, stirring constantly. Add the cognac and wine and stir. Once these have been absorbed, start to add the fish stock, as for the previous risotto recipes.

4.   When the rice is al dente, add the basil, shellfish, salt and pepper, and the remaining butter. Stir to mix and serve immediately.

Risotto con Pomodori e Basilico
Risotto with Tomatoes and Basil

A very simple recipe made with fresh tomatoes and basil.

2	pounds ripe tomatoes	4	cups dry white wine
5	cups broth, beef, veal or chicken	1½	cups rice, Arborio or Carolina
4	tablespoons butter	½	cup Parmigiano, grated
1	tablespoon olive oil	15	fresh basil leaves
⅓	cup chopped red onion		Black pepper

1.   Drop tomatoes into boiling water for 2 minutes. Peel off skin and squeeze out seeds. Chop pulp coarsely.

2.   In a large sauce pot heat 3 tablespoons each butter and oil then add onions. When onions have wilted, add the tomatoes, with salt and pepper.

3.   Add the rice and coat thoroughly. After a few minutes add some of the stock slowly. Stir the rice. As broth is absorbed, repeat the process. Let rice cook over low heat until just tender.

4.   Add the remaining butter and Parmigiano, salt and pepper to taste. Garnish with fresh basil.

NOTE: Provolone cut into small pieces can be a nice addition at the end.

Risotto con Odori
Rice with Herbs and Butter
Serves 6

10   tablespoons butter, at room temperature
1   teaspoon pressed garlic
2   tablespoons finely chopped fresh basil leaves
4   tablespoons finely chopped fresh parsley (leaves only)

2   cups Arborio rice
6   cups, approximately, hot chicken stock
     Salt and freshly ground black pepper
6   tablespoons freshly grated Pecorino Romano

1.   Melt 6 tablespoons of the butter in a heavy-bottomed saucepan. Add the garlic, basil, and parsley and sauté over low heat for one minute.
2.   Add the rice to the pan and sauté for 4 minutes, stirring constantly. Add the stock as for the previous risotto recipes.
3.   When the rice is al dente, stir in the remaining butter, salt and pepper, and 3 tablespoons of the grated cheese. Stir to mix. Serve immediately with the remaining cheese sprinkled on top.

Risotto con Carciofi e Pepperoni
Rice with Artichoke Hearts and Sweet Red Peppers
Serves 6

6	artichoke hearts	1	cup dry white wine
1	lemon	6	cups, approximately, hot chicken stock
4	tablespoons butter		
1	small onion, finely chopped	2	roasted sweet red peppers, peeled, seeded and coarsely chopped
1	garlic clove, finely chopped		
2	tablespoons finely chopped fresh parsley (leaves only)		Salt and freshly ground black pepper
6	thin slices prosciutto (with fat), finely chopped	½	cup freshly grated Parmigiano
2	cups Arborio rice		

1.   Slice the artichoke hearts into ¼-inch-thick wedges. Place them in a bowl with enough water to cover and the juice of the lemon added. Let stand until ready to use.

2.   Melt the butter in a heavy-bottomed saucepan. Add the onion and garlic and sauté until the onion is translucent. Drain the artichokes and pat them dry with paper towels. Add them to the pan along with the prosciutto and parsley. Lower the heat and sauté for 2 minutes, stirring constantly.

3.   Add the rice and sauté for 2 minutes, stirring constantly. Add the wine and stir until it is absorbed. Add the chicken stock as for the previous risotto recipes.

4.   When the rice is al dente, add the roasted peppers, salt and pepper and Parmigiano. Stir gently to mix and serve immediately.

PESCI E FRUTTI DI MARE
Fish and Shellfish

Provincetown's rich history spanning 370 years has bred a community of uniquely independent people, proud to have been a part of this seafaring town. They have created an atmosphere of freedom and tolerance that has attracted a great many people seeking alternative lifestyles, or just the freedom to be themselves — artists and writers inspired by a sense of solitude and isolation; families escaping the rigors of the city, seeking a healthy environment in which to raise their children; gay and lesbian couples seeking an open lifestyle; young entrepreneurs seizing the chance to run their own businesses; retired professionals who fell in love with the Outer Cape years ago; and people powerfully drawn by the natural beauty of the area and the joy of being part of a genuine community, a true American small town.

GILLIAN DRAKE
The Complete Guide to Povincetown
Reprinted by permission

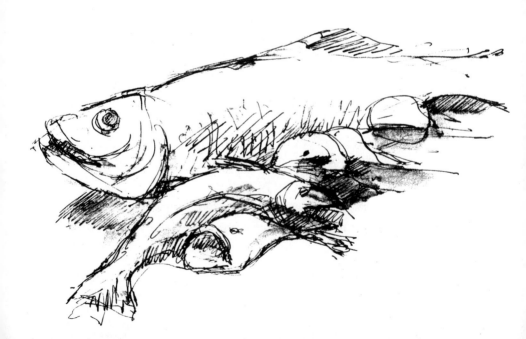

Baccalà con Broccoletti di Rabe
Salt Cod with Broccoli Rabe
Serves 4

1½	pounds salted cod fillets cut in 3-inch sections	18	dry-cured black olives, pitted and chopped
3	tablespoons olive oil	1	teaspoon oregano
	Red pepper flakes to taste	¼	teaspoon anise seed
2	cloves garlic, minced	1½	pounds broccoli rabe,
¾	cup dry white wine		stemmed, cleaned, and blanched

1.   In refrigerator, soak fish in water to cover for two days, changing water frequently. Rinse and dry.

2.   Place cod in ovenproof dish, add oil and red pepper, place in pre-heated 500-degree oven, and lower heat immediately to 325 degrees. Bake for 10 minutes.

3.   When moisture has cooked out, add garlic, wine, olives, oregano and anise. Arrange blanched rabe around cod in pan. Bake for an additional 25 minutes.

NOTE: Salted cod is popular in Italy and Spain. The salting process preserves the fish and "cooks" it, too. Soaking removes the salt and returns the fish to its original tenderness and delicacy.

Sogliola con Finocchio
Flounder Fillets with Fennel
Serves 2

4	tablespoons butter	½	cup dry white wine
2	small fillets of flounder	1	tablespoon dried dill
1	medium fennel bulb	1	teaspoon fennel seed
1	tablespoon butter		Salt and pepper

1.   Cut fennel crosswise in ½-inch strips. Sauté fennel in 1 tablespoon butter until lightly browned.
2.   Remove fennel, add remaining butter and fillets. Cook for 5 minutes, then add wine, dill, and fennel seed and cook 5 minutes more.
3.   Remove fillets to a platter and keep warm. Over high heat, reduce sauce by half, season with salt and pepper and spoon over fish. Garnish with fennel sprigs.

NOTE: Fennel and fish is a classic flavor combination, well known to the French and the Greeks, as well as the Italians.

Pesce alla Giosue
Poached Fish and Clams with White Wine and Herbs
Serves 4

4	tablespoons olive oil	Pinch of hot red pepper flakes
3	garlic cloves, finely chopped	
5	shallots, finely chopped	Pinch of dried rosemary or chopped fresh rosemary
4	1¼-inch-thick striped bass steaks	2 tablespoons chopped fresh chives
12	littleneck clams	
1¼	cups dry white wine	Salt and freshly ground black pepper
¾	cup fish stock (page 67)	
1¼	teaspoons dried basil or chopped fresh basil leaves	

1.   Heat the oil in a skillet. Add the garlic and shallots and sauté until they are golden.
2.   Add the fish and all the remaining ingredients. Cover the pan and poach the fish for about 10 minutes, or until it is done.
3.   Transfer the fish to a warm serving dish. Cook the sauce over high heat to reduce it slightly, then pour over the fish.

NOTE: This sauce is excellent served over spaghetti or linguine. Simply cook the pasta while the fish is poaching. Pour half of the sauce over the fish steaks and the remainder over the pasta.

Spiegola con Vongole
Stiped Bass with Little Neck Clams
Serves 8

3   dozen little neck clams
⅓   cup virgin olive oil
½   cup dry white wine
½   cup chopped whole scallions
2   large gloves of garlic, minced
¼   cup chopped Italian parsley

¼   cup chopped fresh basil
     Salt and pepper
4   pounds striped bass steaks,
     1-inch thick
¼   cup fresh bread crumbs,
     crusts removed

1.   Scrub clams well. Place in a deep pot with a tablespoon of oil and half the wine. Cover and cook, stirring occasionally, just until all shells are opened. Uncover and allow to cool. Remove meat from shells and chop coarse. Reserve the clam broth.

2.   Heat the remaining oil in a pan and add the scallions. After a few minutes, add garlic. When lightly browned, add parsley, basil and wine. Turn up heat and reduce by two-thirds. Add clam broth and reduce by two-thirds again, then add clams.

3.   Preheat oven to 425 degrees. Place fish in a baking pan and season with salt and pepper. Pour clam mixture over fish and then top with bread crumbs.

4.   Bake fish for 10 minutes. Baste with juices while cooking. Remove steaks from pan and place on a heated platter. If pan juices are too thin, reduce over high heat, then pour over fish.

NOTE: Striped bass is sometimes hard to find. Halibut or snapper can be used for this dish.

Spigola alla Procidana
Striped Bass Broiled with Red Wine Vinegar and Mint
Serves 4

8	tablespoons olive oil	1	teaspoon dried oregano
½	cup red wine vinegar		Salt and freshly ground pepper
½	cup dry white wine	4	10-ounce striped bass steaks
3	teaspoons dried basil	8	whole fresh mint leaves

1.   Preheat the broiler.

2.   Combine the first 6 ingredients in a shallow, ovenproof pan. Add the fish to the pan, then lay 2 mint leaves on each steak.

3.   Broil the bass on both sides until it is done. Transfer the steaks to a warm serving dish and pour the sauce over them. Garnish with additional fresh mint sprigs.

Pesce al Forno
Whole Bluefish Baked with Garlic, Rosemary and Basil
Serves 12 to 16

1	8-pound whole bluefish	3	cups extra virgin olive oil
	Salt and freshly ground	2	heads garlic, finely
	black pepper		chopped
8	sprigs fresh rosemary	1	small bunch fresh parsley,
3	bunches fresh basil		finely chopped

1.   Preheat the oven to 375 degrees.

2.   Scale and gut the fish. Then wash it thoroughly, inside and out, in cold water. Rub salt and pepper into the cavity, and stuff with 3 rosemary sprigs and 1 bunch of basil.

3.   Pour the olive oil into a baking pan large enough to hold the fish. Add the garlic, parsley, salt and pepper. Chop the remaining basil and add it to the oil. Stir well. Lay the fish on the oil and roll it around once to coat it with the seasoned oil. Lay the 5 remaining rosemary sprigs over the fish. Cover the pan with aluminum foil and bake for 40 to 45 minutes.

4.   To serve, lift the skin off the top side of the fish. Cut down to the bone, making rectangular portions. Lift each portion off the bones with a narrow spatula. Spoon a little of the oil and herbs from the pan over each portion. Turn the fish over and repeat the process to serve from the other side.

Filetti di Pesce al Possillipo
Fish Sautéed with Mixed Vegetables
Serves 6

2	pounds striped bass or red snapper fillets, cut into 3-inch pieces	5	tablespoons olive oil
½	cup diced fennel bulb	½	teaspoon fresh rosemary
½	cup diced carrots	½	teaspoon oregano
½	cup diced celery		black pepper and salt
½	cup diced red onion	4	drops hot pepper sauce
2	tablespoons butter	1	cup red wine, (Zinfandel, Merlot, etc.)
		8	lemon slices for garnish

1.   In a large saute skillet heat 1 tablespoon of butter and the oil over moderate heat. Add the vegetables. Cook and stir until vegetables start browning. Transfer cooked vegetables to a plate. Return oil to pan, then add remaining butter.

2.   Dry fish and dust with flour. Shake off excess. Place fish in pan when oil is hot, not smoking. Brown on both sides. Add salt and pepper.

3.   Remove fish, return vegetables to pan, add wine and herbs. Reduce liquid to half. Place fish back in skillet. Cook over low heat 5 or 6 minutes. Place fish on warm platter and surround with vegetables. Garnish with lemon slices and fresh herbs.

Pesce alla Sardenese
Fish Sautéed with Green Pepper and Coriander
Serves 4

2	tablespoons olive oil	4	tomatoes, peeled, seeded and chopped
1	onion, sliced into thin rounds		
1	sweet green pepper, seeded and sliced very thin	2	teaspoons finely chopped fresh parsley leaves
4	8-ounce haddock, halibut, flounder or bass fillets	2	teaspoons chopped fresh coriander leaves
	Juice of 1 lime		Salt and freshly ground black pepper
½	cup dry white wine		

1.   Heat the oil in a large skillet. Add the onion and sauté for 5 minutes. Add the green pepper and sauté for 3 to 4 minutes. Remove the vegetables from the pan and set them aside.

2.   Raise the heat and add the fish to the pan. Sauté for several minutes on each side (the cooking time will depend on the thickness of the fish). Return the vegetables to the pan and add the remaining ingredients; reduce for 1 minute.

3.   Transfer the fish to warm serving plates and garnish with the vegetables and some of the sauce. Serve immediately.

Pesce con Salsa Verde
Broiled Halibut with Green Sauce
Serves 4

¼ cup fresh bread crumbs made from crustless bread

2 tablespoons red wine vinegar

¼ cup extra virgin olive oil
   juice of ½ lemon

½ cup fresh basil leaves

½ cup fresh parsley leaves

10 anchovy fillets, rinsed and dried

2 hard-boiled large egg yolks
   Salt and freshly ground black pepper

4 10-ounce skinless halibut fillets

1 large garlic clove, sliced in half
   Juice of 1 lemon
   Coarsely ground black pepper

¼ cup extra virgin olive oil
   Salt

1. Preheat the broiler.

2. Prepare the Salsa Verde: Soak the bread crumbs in the wine vinegar. Squeeze all the excess vinegar out of the bread crumbs and then combine them with the next 7 ingredients in a food processor or blender and blend until smooth.

3. Rub the halibut fillets with the garlic, lemon juice and coarsely ground black pepper. (Reserve some of the lemon juice.) Place the fillets in an ovenproof dish. Sprinkle them with the remaining lemon juice, olive oil and salt. Broil until done, turning the fillets once. Just before the fillets are done, place 2 tablespoons of the Salsa Verde on each fillet. Return them to the broiler for a moment and serve immediately.

Sogliola Semplice
Sole Sautéed with Shallots and Scallions
Serves 4

⅓ cup olive oil
3 garlic cloves, finely chopped
4 shallots, finely chopped
6 scallions, white and green
   parts, sliced on the diagonal
4 10-ounce sole or flounder
   fillets
1½ cups thinly sliced fresh
    mushrooms

2 tablespoons dry vermouth
   Juice of 1 lemon
2 teaspoons finely chopped
   fresh parsley
   Salt and freshly ground
   black pepper
   Lemon wedges and parsley
   sprigs for garnish

1.   Heat the oil in a skillet. Add the garlic, shallots and scallions and sauté for 5 minutes, or until the shallots and scallions are translucent. Be careful not to burn the garlic.
2.   Add all the remaining ingredients, except the lemon wedges and parsley sprigs, and cook the fillets over medium heat until they are opaque.
3.   Transfer the fillets to a warm serving dish and pour the vegetables and sauce over them. Garnish with the lemon wedges and parsley sprigs.

Sogliola di Nozze
Poached Sole with Tarragon and Sour Cream Sauce
Serves 4

⅓ cup clarified butter (page 309)

½ cup dry white wine

Juice of 1 lemon

4 10-ounce sole or flounder fillets

1 teaspoon chopped fresh tarragon leaves

Salt and freshly ground black pepper

1 cup sour cream, at room temperature, and whipped to a more liquid consistency

3 tablespoons chopped fresh chives

1.   Heat the butter in a skillet. Add the wine, lemon juice, fish and tarragon. Season with a little salt and pepper. Cover the pan and poach the fish over low heat just until the fish becomes opaque.

2.   Transfer the fish to a warm serving dish. Return the liquid in the skillet to a boil and whisk in the sour cream and chives. Do not boil after sour cream is added. If necessary, add more salt and pepper. Pour the sauce over the fillets and serve immediately.

Sogliola alla Primavera
Sautéed Sole with Vegetable Puree
Serves 4

2   cups peeled and seeded ripe
     tomatoes
½   cup chopped carrots
½   cup chopped zucchini
2   shallots, peeled
⅓   cup clarified butter
     (page 309)
1   bay leaf
2   pounds sole or flounder fillets

½   cup dry white wine
⅓   cup fish stock (page 67)
½   teaspoon dried thyme or
     chopped fresh thyme leaves
     Salt and freshly ground
     black pepper
2   scallions, thinly sliced on the
     diagonal

1.   Combine the tomatoes, carrot, zucchini and shallots in a food processor and process until finely chopped.
2.   Heat half the butter in a skillet and add the chopped vegetables and bay leaf. Cook over low heat for 12 minutes. Press the vegetables through a coarse sieve, then set them aside.
3.   In the same skillet, heat the remaining butter. Add the fish, wine, stock, thyme, salt and pepper. Cover and poach the fish just until it becomes opaque.
4.   Transfer the fish to a warm serving dish. Add the vegetables to the skillet and stir to mix. Cook for 2 minutes to reduce the sauce. Pour the sauce over the fish and garnish with the scallions.

Brodetto di Pesce
Fish Stew with Tomatoes and Herbs
Serves 4

¼	cup olive oil	1	tablespoon chopped fresh basil leaves
2	garlic cloves, finely chopped		
4	shallots, finely chopped	1	bay leaf
4	1¼-inch-thick cod, bass or bluefish steaks	2	teaspoons finely chopped fresh parsley leaves
12	littleneck clams, washed		Salt and freshly ground black pepper
¼	cup dry red wine		
¼	cup dry white wine		Chopped fresh parsley or basil leaves for garnish
1½	cups Marinara Sauce (page 116)		

1.   Heat the oil in a large skillet. Add the garlic and shallots and sauté until they are golden.

2.   Add the fish, clams, red and white wines. Cover the pan and bring to a boil, then lower the heat and simmer for 3 minutes. Add the remaining ingredients, cover the pan again and simmer until done, about 10 minutes.

3.   Transfer the fish to a warm serving platter and arrange the clams around it. Pour the sauce over the fish and clams and garnish with chopped fresh parsley or basil leaves.

NOTE: The brodetto is excellent served with spaghetti that has been sauced with some of the brodetto. Garlic croutons are also an excellent accompaniment. (Arrange the croutons around the fish and pour sauce over them.)

To make the croutons, slice a thin loaf of french bread on the diagonal (the slices should be ¼-inch-thick). Drizzle extra virgin olive oil over each slice and sprinkle with salt. Bake in a 400 degree oven until golden. Rub both sides of each slice with a split clove of garlic. Serve immediately.

Pesce Misto
Mixed Fish Poached with Tomatoes and Pernod
Serves 4 to 6

1	cup olive oil
2	garlic cloves, finely chopped
1	medium-size onion, minced
2	celery stalks, finely chopped
1	cup fish stock (page 67)
1	cup dry white wine
¼	cup chopped fresh tarragon
¼	cup fennel seeds, crushed
¼	teaspoon ground turmeric
⅛	teaspoon black pepper
4	ripe tomatoes, peeled, seed-ed and chopped
1	tablespoon Pernod
½	cup finely chopped parsley
16	mussels, scrubbed and debearded
12	littleneck clams, washed
8	shrimp, shelled and deveined
1	pound haddock or bluefish
6	soft-shelled crabs, cleaned and dredged in flour

1.   Preheat the oven to 400 degrees.

2.   Heat half of the oil in a deep skillet. Add the garlic, onion and celery and sauté for 5 minutes. Add the stock, wine, tarragon, fennel, turmeric and black pepper. Simmer for 10 minutes and then add the tomatoes, parsley and Pernod. Simmer 5 minutes.

3.   Add the mussels and clams to the pan, cover and cook over moderate to high heat until they have opened. Remove and set aside.

4.   To the same skillet add the fish and shrimp. Leave only enough sauce in the pan to poach the fish. (Reserve the extra sauce.) Cover the pan and poach the fish over low heat just until they are cooked.

5.   Heat the remaining oil in another skillet and sauté the soft-shelled crabs for about 3 minutes on each side, or until brown.

6.   Combine all the seafood except the crabs in a large ovenproof serving dish. Pour a generous amount of the sauce over the seafood but do not make it a soup. Place the crabs on top and cover the dish with aluminum foil. Bake until all the ingredients are well heated.

*S*ome days friends would come by the restaurant with fish or other foods to make dinner for the "gang. " One day artist and friend Edward Giobbi prepared a dish with fish, shellfish and chicken. Everyone loved it. It was 1957, the year that the Chrysler Museum opened in Provincetown, and Walter Chrysler was having a dinner party at the restaurant for fifty people. The guests included Hudson Walker, the founder of the Fine Arts Work Center, and the artist Seong Moy. With Eddie's help, Ciro and Sal prepared the Cacciucco for all fifty people. It was so well received by the guests that they decided to keep it on the menu. It is there to this day.

Cacciucco alla Livornese
Fish Stew with Capers and Fresh Herbs
Serves 4

1	1½-pound chicken, cut into 10 or 12 pieces	1	teaspoon chopped fresh rosemary leaves
½	cup olive oil	2	tablespoons finely chopped fresh parsley leaves
3	garlic cloves, peeled		
¼	cup red wine vinegar	1	1¾-pounds lobster
¼	cup dry white wine	8	littleneck clams, washed
	Salt and freshly ground black pepper	12	mussels, washed and debearded
3	cups Marinara Sauce (page 116)	1	pound haddock or cod
1	tablespoon capers, rinsed and drained	8	shrimp, shelled and deveined
		2	squid, cleaned and sliced into ¼-inch rings
1	tablespoon chopped fresh basil leaves		

1.   Preheat the oven to 400 degrees.

2.   Heat the oil in a skillet. Add the chicken and the garlic and brown the chicken on both sides. Lower the heat and add the vinegar, wine, salt and pepper. Cook until the chicken is almost done then remove and set aside. Discard the garlic.

3.   Add the Marinara sauce, capers, basil, rosemary and 1 tablespoon of the parsley to the skillet. Simmer for 5 minutes.

4.   Transfer the sauce to a roasting pan and add the lobster, clams and mussels to the pan. Place the pan over two burners on top of the stove. Cover the pan and cook for 15 minutes.

5.   Place the fish, shrimp and squid in another skillet. Add 1 cup of the sauce from the lobster pan. Cover the skillet and cook over medium heat, being careful not to overcook. The fish and shellfish should be slightly

underdone.

6.   Combine the chicken, fish, shrimp and squid in the roasting pan with the lobster, clams and mussels. Cover the pan with aluminum foil and bake for 10 minutes.

7.   Remove the pan from the oven. Crack the lobster claws and split the tail. Arrange the remaining seafood and chicken on a large serving dish. Arrange the lobster pieces on top and pour about 2 cups of the sauce over all. Sprinkle the remaining tablespoon of parsley on top.

Baccalà Semplice
Simple Salt Cod
Serves 6

2	pounds salt cod	½	cup extra virgin olive oil
3	garlic cloves, peeled		Freshly ground black pepper
2	parsley sprigs		

1.   Soak the salt cod in abundant cold water for 24 hours, changing the water often. Remove it from the water and rinse it with fresh cold water. Remove the skin and trim away any excess fat or bones. Divide the fish into 6 portions.

2.   Put the cod in a large casserole. Add the garlic, parsley and 3 table-spoons of the olive oil. Cover the cod with cold water and bring to a boil, then lower the heat and simmer for 20 minutes.

3.   Transfer the cod to warm serving plates. Drizzle the cod with a gen-erous amount of olive oil and sprinkle with pepper.

Pesce in Umido
Fish Stewed with Anchovies, Capers and Fresh Herbs
Serves 4

¼   cup olive oil
3   garlic cloves, finely chopped
4   anchovy fillets, rinsed, dried and chopped
4   10-ounce bluefish or cod steaks
2   tablespoons dry red wine
1   cup dry white wine
1   tablespoon red wine vinegar
1   tablespoon capers, rinsed and drained
1   tablespoon chopped fresh basil leaves
½   teaspoon dried oregano
½   teaspoon chopped fresh rosemary leaves
2   teaspoons finely chopped fresh parsley leaves
¼   teaspoon hot red pepper flakes
4   slices ripe tomato
1½   cups Marinara Sauce (page 116)
    Parsley sprigs for garnish

1.   Heat the oil in a large skillet. Add the garlic and anchovies and sauté until the garlic is golden and the anchovies have dissolved (mash them with a fork).

2.   Add all the remaining ingredients, except the Marinara sauce, to the pan. The tomato slices should be placed on the fish steaks. Cover the pan and cook the fish over low heat for 3 minutes.

3.   Add the Marinara sauce to the pan and simmer until the fish is done, about 8 minutes.

4.   Transfer to a warm serving dish and garnish with the parsley sprigs.

Baccalà in Umido alla Genovina
Genovina's Stewed Salt Cod with Potatoes
Serves 6

2	pounds salt cod	4	plum tomatoes, peeled, seeded and chopped
¼	cup olive oil		
1	onion, finely chopped	2	parsley sprigs
1	garlic clove, finely chopped		Freshly ground black pepper
2	pounds white potatoes, peeled and cut into ¼-inch wedges		

1.   Soak the salt cod in abundant cold water for 24 hours, changing the water often. Remove it from the water and rinse it in cold water. Remove the skin and trim away any excess fat or bones. Cut into pieces approximately 2- x 1-inch.

2.   Heat the olive oil in a heavy casserole. Add the onions and garlic and sauté until the onion is translucent. Add the potatoes, lower the heat and cook for 10 minutes.

3.   Add the salt cod, tomatoes, parsley and pepper. Stir gently. If the stew seems too dry, add a little white wine or water. Cover the pot and cook slowly for 20 minutes.

Conchiglie e Animelle
Scallops and Sweetbreads Sautéed
with Fresh Morels and Madeira
Serves 4

1   pound sweetbreads
1   celery stalk, chopped
1   onion, chopped
½   carrot, chopped
2   tablespoons red wine vinegar
     Salt and freshly ground black
     pepper
2   tablespoons clarified butter
     (page 309)

1   tablespoon finely chopped
     shallots
1   pound sea scallops
¼   cup dry Madeira
½   pound fresh morels (or sliced
     fresh mushrooms)
2 to 4 tablespoons sweet butter,
     softened

1.   Remove the fat and tubes from the sweetbreads. Cover them with cold water to which a little salt has been added. Soak for 1 to 2 hours, then drain.

2.   Put the sweetbreads in a saucepan. Cover with cold water and add the celery, onion, carrot, vinegar, salt and pepper. Bring to a boil, then lower the heat and simmer for 5 minutes. Drain and cool under cold running water. Cut the sweetbreads into ¼-inch-thick slices, removing any membranes or connective tissue.

3.   Heat the butter in a large skillet. Add the shallots and sauté for 1 minute (do not burn). Add the scallops and sauté for 2 minutes, then add the mushrooms and sauté for another 2 minutes. Add the sweetbreads and stir gently. Add the Madeira and move the pan in quick circular motions to facilitate the reduction of the wine, about 1 to 2 minutes.

4.   Remove the scallops and sweetbreads to a warm serving dish.

5.   Whisk the butter quickly into the sauce and season with salt and pepper. Pour the sauce over the scallops and sweetbreads. Serve immediately.

Conchiglie al Gimignano
Scallops Broiled with Mushrooms and Madeira
Serves 4

1½	pounds sea or bay scallops		Juice of ½ lemon
1	cup thinly sliced fresh	2	garlic cloves, pressed
	mushrooms		Salt and freshly ground black
½	cup olive oil		pepper
½	cup Madeira		

1. Preheat the broiler.
2. In a shallow, ovenproof pan combine the scallops, mushrooms, oil, wine, lemon juice, garlic, salt and pepper.
3. Place the pan under the broiler (it should be 2 inches from the heat source) and cook for 5 to 6 minutes, turning the scallops once. Be careful not to overcook them.
4. Transfer the scallops to a warm serving dish and pour the sauce over them. Serve immediately.

Zuppa di Vongole
Clams Cooked with Wine and Herbs
Serves 4

½   cup olive oil
4   garlic cloves, finely chopped
8   shallots, finely chopped
½   cup dry red wine
½   cup dry white wine
2   tablespoons dried basil or chopped fresh basil leaves

1   teaspoon hot red pepper flakes
    2 tablespoons finely chopped fresh parsley leaves
48 littleneck clams, washed
2   cups Marinara Sauce (page 116)

1.   Heat the oil in a large deep saucepan or rondo. Add the garlic and shallots and sauté until they are golden. Add all the remaining ingredients, cover the pan and cook over moderate heat until all the clams have opened.
2.   Arrange the clams in a serving bowl and pour the sauce over them.

Cozze al Cozzi
Mussels Poached in White Wine and Herbs
Serves 4

2 tablespoons olive oil
2 garlic cloves, finely chopped
¼ cup dry white wine
1 teaspoon dried basil or chopped fresh basil leaves
¼ teaspoon dried oregano
¼ teaspoon hot red pepper flakes
1 tablespoon finely chopped fresh parsley leaves
   Salt and freshly ground black pepper
40 mussels, scrubbed and debearded

1.   Heat the olive oil in a large saucepan. Add the garlic and sauté until it is golden. Add the remaining ingredients, cover the pan and simmer gently until all the mussels have opened, about 7 minutes.

2.   Arrange the mussels on a large serving dish or in a large bowl and pour the sauce over them. Serve immediately.

Calamari e Aranci con Balsamico
Squid and Orange with Balsamic Vinegar
Serves 6

¾   cup virgin olive oil
2½   pounds squid, cleaned
2   large red onions, sliced in eights
2   blood oranges, sliced ¼-inch thick
2   celery hearts, chopped

¼   cup balsamic vinegar
¼   cup fresh orange juice
½   cup fresh chervil
¼   teaspoon coriander
1   large clove garlic, minced
     Salt and black pepper

If a grill is not available, use a broiler.

1.   Toss squid, onion and orange slices in oil. Grill the squid for approximately 2 minutes and tentacles for another minute. Grill onions and oranges for 4 to 5 minutes. When squid has cooled, cut bodies into rings. Leave tentacles whole. Chop onions coarse.

2.   Mix all ingredients, squid, onions, orange slices, juice, etc., in a bowl. Toss gently and chill for 1 to 2 hours before serving.

Scampi con Salsa di Pepperoni
Scampi with Pepper Sauce
Serves 4

1	recipe Pepper Sauce, (page 120)	½	teaspoon rosemary
1	pound shrimp, 16-20 count, peeled, deveined, tails on	2	large shallots
2	teaspoons olive oil	½	cup scallions
¼	cup fresh basil	1	tablespoon balsamic vinegar
		2	large cloves garlic, minced

1.   In a skillet heat olive oil. When hot, add shrimp, toss quickly, add all other ingredients except Pepper Sauce. Cook for 5 minutes.

2.   Remove shrimp and keep warm. Add Pepper Sauce to pan. Cook until hot.

3.   Place some sauce on heated platter, arrange shrimp with tails out. Garnish with fresh basil and rosemary.

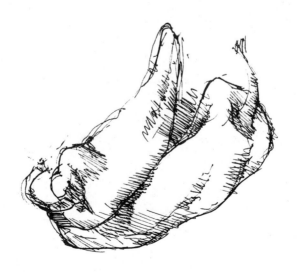

Scampi alla Griglia
Shrimp Broiled with Scallions and Butter
Serves 4

1⅓ cups clarified butter (page309)
⅔ cup olive oil
2 garlic cloves, peeled
2 small onions, chopped
Juice of 1 lemon
Salt and freshly ground black pepper

6 scallions, white and green parts, thinly sliced on the diagonal
28 large shrimp, shelled and deveined.

1.   Preheat the broiler.
2.   Combine the butter, oil, garlic, onion, lemon juice, salt and pepper in a bowl and blend thoroughly with a whisk.
3.   Put the shrimp in a shallow ovenproof pan and sprinkle the scallions over them. Pour the butter and oil mixture over the shrimp. Put the pan under the broiler (3 inches from the heat source) and broil for about 3 minutes on each side.
4.   Transfer the shrimp to a warm serving dish and pour the sauce over them.

Aragosta Piccante al Ciro
Lobster with Piquant Sauce
Serves 4

2	2-pound live lobsters	2	tablespoons tomato paste
¼	cup olive oil	1	teaspoon chopped fresh
¾	cup coarsely chopped shallots		rosemary leaves
8	anchovy fillets, rinsed and	1	teaspoon chopped fresh sage
	chopped		leaves
4	garlic cloves, finely chopped		Coarsely ground black pepper
½	cup dry red wine	4	tablespoons red wine vinegar
1	cup fish stock (page 67)	¼	cup finely chopped fresh
½	cup Dijon mustard		parsley leaves

1.   Prepare the lobsters: Pierce them through the head to kill them; crack the claws, legs and knuckles and split the tails.

2.   Heat the oil in a large pan and sauté the lobster pieces over high heat for 10 minutes. Add the shallots, anchovies, garlic, wine and stock. Lower the heat and simmer for 10 minutes.

3.   Stir in the mustard, tomato paste, rosemary, sage and black pepper. Cover and cook for 5 minutes more. Add the vinegar and half of the parsley.

4.   Remove the lobster and cook the sauce over low heat for 20 minutes.

5.   Using lobster shears cut away the top half of the claws. Cut the undersides of the tails and spread them open. Do the same with the knuckles. Leave all the lobster meat in the shells. Arrange the lobster, reproducing its true shape, on a warm platter. Place in a warm (250 degree) oven, if necessary, until the sauce is ready.

6.   Spoon the sauce over the lobster and sprinkle with the remaining parsley.

Moleche di San Gennaro
Soft-Shell Crabs Sautéed
with White Wine and Lemon
Serves 4

16	soft-shelled crabs	6	shallots, finely chopped
½	cup all-purpose flour		Juice of ½ lemon
	Salt and freshly ground black	½	cup dry white wine
	pepper	3	tablespoons finely chopped
1	cup clarified butter (page 309)		fresh parsley leaves
4	garlic cloves, finely chopped	8	thin lemon slices for garnish

1.   Clean the crabs: Pierce them between the eyes with a knife, lift the pointed ends of the shells and scrape out the spongy portion between the shell and the body. Put the crabs on their backs and cut off the flaps on the bottom sides. Wash them thoroughly in cold water and dry completely.

2.   Combine the flour with a little salt and pepper in a shallow pan. Dredge the crabs in the flour and shake off any excess.

3.   Heat the butter in a large skillet and sauté the crabs until they are brown and crisp on one side. Turn them over and add the garlic and shallots to the pan. Sauté until the crabs are brown and crisp on the second side, being careful not to burn the garlic and shallots.

4.   Transfer the crabs to a warm serving plate. Add the lemon juice, wine and parsley to the pan and cook over high heat for about 2 minutes. Pour the sauce over the crabs and garnish with the lemon slices.

Pesce Adriatico
Poached Fish and Shellfish with Caper-Butter Sauce
Serves 4

4	7-ounce haddock fillets or halibut steaks		Generous splash of red wine vinegar
24	mussels, washed and debearded	2	teaspoons chopped fresh rosemary leaves
12	shrimp, shelled and deveined	1	teaspoon dried thyme
2	tablespoons capers, rinsed and drained		Salt and freshly ground black pepper
½	cup dry white wine	10	tablespoons butter, softened

1.   Place all the ingredients, except 8 tablespoons of the butter, into a large saucepan (if necessary, use 2 pans). Cover the pan and bring to a boil.
2.   Lower the heat and simmer until the mussels have opened and the fish is flaky.
3.   Remove the fish and shellfish to a warm serving platter. Add the butter to the pan and whisk it rapidly into the sauce. Season with more salt and pepper. Pour the sauce over the fish and shellfish and serve immediately.

POLLO
Chicken

There are certain moments, certain places, that stick in your mind, that become guide-lines, the ultimate experience that all others are compared with, and, of course, fall short of.

I spent my first twelve summers in Provincetown on Cape Cod. My father worked with a fellow up there named Peter Hunt who owned a whole alleyway of shops. One sum-mer, a little coffee and sandwich place—an outdoor cafe—appeared in the alley. My only interest in it was that my "boyfriend's" mother worked there. It was owned by two artists, Ciro Cozzi and Sal Del Deo. Shortly after they opened up, I stopped going to Provincetown. I was a teenager and wanted to stay in Brooklyn with the guys and go to Coney Island.

I went back to Provincetown when I was about eighteen. My father gave me fifty dol-lars to rent a bike, buy flipper dough and eat at Ciro and Sal's on Wednesday night. The spe-cial was "Cacciucco Livornese"— whole lobster, chicken, cherrystone clams, mussels and other varieties of seafood, baked in a light sauce of tomato, wine and herbs, en casserole. Being a dutiful daughter and mostly because my father knew what was good, I went—down the old Peter Hunt Alley, into a courtyard, down a few stone steps, into a tiny room sparkling with candles, and filled with the most wonderful smells my nose had ever encountered. I sat down at a tiny table on a very uncomfortable nail keg and ordered the special. What happened after that is history. I've never forgotten that meal. It was one of the first I had had the plea-sure of eating

alone and uninterrupted. I closed my eyes, I rocked in ecstasy; I sucked on mussel shells and rolled rice and sauce around in my mouth. It was heaven. I remember discussing the food with my sister, who had done the same thing. We were in awe.

Then a few more years passed. I opened and closed my first restaurant. And one April evening I found myself back in Provincetown. I went to Ciro's. It was bigger, and they had a liquor license, but the smells were the same—wonderful. I went upstairs and sat alone in a corner. I ordered a bottle of wine, a pile of steamed mussels and an order of fried zucchini. Life once again took on new dimensions. I asked the waiter—Dennis was his name—how the veal was. "We are famous for our veal." Great! I ordered another bottle of wine, and "Veal Piccata— scallops of veal with mushrooms, lemon and cream." Dennis thought it was too much. "Don't worry, sweetheart, I can handle it."

After dinner I was in seventh heaven, a bit crocked, and I sent a note down to the kitchen. I don't remember now the exact wording, but it was a love note. I wrote that I had eaten there when I was younger, and I had never forgotten it. Since then I had opened a restaurant myself and was inspired by Ciro and Sal's. I signed it "Alice of Alice's Restaurant," something I had never done before.

Dennis came back up with my brandy, followed by Ciro and everybody else who worked there. There was lots of brandy and laughing and hugging and smiling and kissing as Ciro and I talked about veal with such zeal that we finally lunged at each other across the table, screaming ravioli, cannelloni and spinach noodles, and zuppa di pesce. All in all, it was a wonderful meeting.

Thank you, Ciro and Sal's.

ALICE MAY BROCK
Reprinted from *My Life as a Restaurant*

Pollo Arrosto con Patate e Rosmarino

Roast Chicken with Potatoes and Rosemary

Serves 4

1	3-pound chicken, cut into quarters, washed and trimmed of excess fat	1	cup olive oil
		1	tablespoon chopped fresh rosemary leaves
1	garlic clove, cut in half Salt and freshly ground black pepper	4	Idaho potatoes, washed and dried

1.   Preheat the oven to 375 degrees.

2.   Rub the chicken pieces on all sides with the garlic, salt, pepper and some of the olive oil. Sprinkle with 2 teaspoons of the rosemary.

3.   Rub some of the oil over the bottom of a large roasting pan. Arrange the chicken quarters, skin side up, in the center of the pan.

4.   Slice the potatoes into ½-inch wedges. Put the potatoes in a bowl and pour the remaining oil over them. Toss well to coat the potatoes completely with the oil. Arrange the potatoes around the chicken. They should be arranged, skin side down, one next to the other, not overlapping. Sprinkle the potatoes with salt, pepper and the remaining rosemary.

5.   Bake uncovered for 1 hour or until the chicken is done. Baste the chicken frequently with its own juices. When done, the potatoes will be crispy outside and fluffy inside.

Pollo alla Bolognese
Roasted Chicken with a Brandy-Cream Sauce
Serves 4 to 6

1	3-pound chicken, cut into 4 or 6 pieces	6	tablespoons butter
¼	cup olive oil	1	cup thinly sliced fresh mushrooms
1	garlic glove, cut in half	1	carrot, finely chopped
1	teaspoon dried tarragon or chopped fresh tarragon leaves	1	celery stalk, finely chopped
	Salt and freshly ground black pepper	1	medium-size onion, finely chopped
¾	cup dry white wine	½	teaspoon dried thyme
¼	cup dry sherry	1	garlic clove, finely chopped
¼	cup brandy	½	cup chicken stock (page 65)
		½	cup heavy cream

1.   Preheat the oven to 350 degrees. Coat the bottom of a roasting pan with half the oil.

2.   Rub the chicken pieces with the remaining oil and the garlic halves, then sprinkle each piece with the tarragon, salt and pepper. Arrange the chicken, skin side up, in the baking pan. Bake uncovered for 45 minutes or until done. Baste the chicken with ½ cup of the white wine, ¼ cup sherry and 3 tablespoons of the brandy throughout the baking period. Drain the fat from the pan, reserving the chicken juices.

3.   While the chicken is cooking prepare the vegetables.
Heat 3 tablespoons of the butter in a skillet and sauté the mushrooms until they are tender. Season them with salt and pepper, then remove the mushrooms to a warm plate and cover to keep them warm.

4.   In the same pan, heat the remaining 3 tablespoons of butter and sauté the carrot, celery and onion until they are tender. Add the thyme, salt and pepper to taste. Cover and set aside.

5.   Prepare the sauce. Pour the remaining wine and brandy into a hot skillet, bring to a boil and cook off the alcohol. Add the chopped garlic, stock, salt and pepper to taste, and simmer for 3 minutes. Add the juices from the baking pan (about ¼ cup), and the heavy cream and simmer for 5 minutes.

6.   Arrange the chicken pieces on a warm serving platter. Arrange the carrot, celery, and onion mixture around the chicken. Sprinkle the mushrooms over the chicken. Pour the sauce over all and serve immediately.

Pollo con Melanzane
Chicken Breast with Eggplant
Serves 1

SAUCE

4	tablespoons canola oil		2	large shallots, chopped fine
½	cup chopped sun dried tomatoes, soaked in warm water		1	teaspoon crushed rosemary
			⅓	cup red wine

1	chicken breast, skinless, boneless			Salt and pepper
4	slices eggplant, ¼-inch-thick rounds		4	tablespoons olive oil
			1	tablespoon pesto
2	slices prosciutto		2	tablespoons Parmigiano, coarsely grated

1.   Saute the shallots in 2 tablespoons canola oil. Add the sun dried tomatoes, cook over low heat for 5 minutes, then add wine. Add rosemary, salt and pepper and simmer for 20 minutes. Set aside.

2.   Lightly pound chicken breast, season with salt and pepper. Brown chicken on both sides in 2 tablespoons of canola oil.

3.   Brush eggplant rounds with olive oil. Place under broiler until brown on both sides. Remove and set aside.

4.   Assembly: Place a small amount of wine sauce in center of an oven-proof dish. Place 2 slices of eggplant in the dish, add a slice of prosciutto, a spoonful of sauce and a sprinkling of Parmigiano. Repeat the process until all the eggplant and prosciutto have been used. Place chicken breast on top. Spread a small amount of sauce on breast. Place in a preheated 400-degree oven for 10 minutes. Before serving, make a ring of pesto around chicken on the outer edge of dish. Sprinkle Parmigiano over breast; garnish with sprigs of rosemary.

Pollo all' Arrabbiato
Roast Chicken with Red Pepper
Serves 4 to 8

2   2-pound chickens, cut into quarters
½   cup olive oil
1   garlic clove, cut in half
1¼   teaspoons cayenne pepper
      Salt and freshly ground black pepper
½   cup dry white wine
8   fresh artichoke hearts
¼   of a fresh lemon
4   tablespoons butter
1½   cups thinly sliced fresh mushrooms
1   cup Espagnole Sauce (page 271)
8   ½-inch slices roasted sweet red peppers

1.   Preheat the oven to 375 degrees. Coat the bottom of a roasting pan with half of the oil.

2.   Rub the chicken with the remaining oil and the garlic halves, then sprinkle each piece with ⅛ teaspoon of the cayenne pepper and some salt and black pepper. Arrange the chicken in the pan and bake uncovered for 50 minutes, or until done. Baste the chicken with the white wine throughout the baking period. Strain the fat from the pan and reserve the juices.

3.   While the chicken is cooking, blanche the artichokes in boiling water with the lemon until they are tender, then drain. Heat the butter in a skillet and sauté the mushrooms until tender, add the artichoke hearts, salt and pepper and mix well. Cover and set aside.

4.   Prepare the sauce: Heat the Espagnole Sauce in a saucepan. Add the juices from the chicken, the remaining ¼ teaspoon of cayenne pepper, salt and pepper. Simmer for 5 minutes.

5.   Stir ¼ cup of the sauce into the pan with the artichokes and mushrooms. Simmer, stirring, for 5 minutes.

6.   Briefly heat the peppers in a separate pan. Arrange the chicken on a warm serving platter. Top the pieces with the roasted red pepper slices.

7.   Arrange the artichoke mixture around the chicken and pour the sauce over all.

Petti di Pollo con Salsa di Pepperoni
Breast of Chicken with Pepper Sauce
Serves 2

2	boneless breasts of chicken	½	cup white wine
2	teaspoons olive oil		black pepper, salt to taste
1	medium red onion, sliced thin	2	tablespoons minced fresh
½	cup minced celery		savory
2	cloves garlic, minced	1	recipe Pepper Sauce
6	green olives, halved		(page 120)

1.   Heat oil in skillet. Place breasts in pan, skin side down, and brown lightly. Add onions, celery and olives. Cook, uncovered, over low heat.

2.   When onion wilts, add remaining ingredients except Pepper Sauce.

3.   Remove skin, return breasts to pan. Add Pepper Sauce. Cook for 10 minutes over low heat. Garnish with parsley.

Pollo al Modo Mio
Chicken My Way
Serves 4

Start this recipe early in the day so you can chill the broth and skim off all the congealed fat.

1	3½ to 4 pound broiler, cut up, skin and fat removed	1	teaspoon marjoram
6	garlic cloves, minced		Salt and pepper
8	sage leaves, minced	½	cup white wine
1	teaspoon rosemary	¼	cup red wine
			Parsley for garnish

1.   Wash chicken and pat dry. Rub chicken with garlic, herbs, salt and pepper and place in a heavy pan. Cook, covered, over low heat for 30 minutes.

2.   Add wine and simmer for 20 minutes. When done, remove chicken and let liquid cool in refrigerator. After liquid has chilled remove fat from surface.

3.   Return all ingredients to pan and heat for 6 minutes. Serve family style. Garnish with parsley and lemon slices.

Pollo al Forno
Roast Stuffed Chicken
Serves 4 to 6

STUFFING

1	tablespoon canola oil		3	tablespoons dried apricots, chopped
1	medium onion, chopped			
¾	cup seasoned bread crumbs		1	tablespoon dry sherry
1	clove garlic, pressed		1	tablespoon sweet sherry
1	teaspoon thyme		2	egg whites (or Egg Beaters)

1	3½ pound chicken			Salt and pepper
1	tablespoon rosemary		½	cup wine vinegar
1	cup Dijon mustard		½	cup water

1. Preheat oven to 500 degrees.
2. Cook onions in oil until wilted, then add rest of stuffing ingredients.
3. Place filling in the cavity of the chicken and truss. Rub chicken with black pepper and salt and smear with mustard. Place on a rack.
4. Pour vinegar and water into pan. Put pan in and lower heat to 375 degrees. Baste chicken often. Roast for approximately 1 hour and 30 minutes. Let rest 20 minutes. Defat pan juices and pass as gravy.

Pollo alla Ravinella
Roast Chicken with Baby Onions
and Carrots in Brown Sauce
Serves 4 to 8

2	2-pound chickens, cut into quarters
¼	cup olive oil
1	garlic clove, cut in half
1½	tablespoons dried rosemary, crushed
	Salt and freshly ground black pepper
⅔	cup dry white wine
⅔	cup Espagnole Sauce (page 271)
¼	cup chicken stock (page 65)
1	tablespoon red wine vinegar
½	teaspoon dry mustard
3	tablespoons butter
1½	cup fresh mushrooms cut into halves
3	carrots, cut into julienne
1½	cups peeled pearl onions

1.   Preheat the oven to 375 degrees. Coat the bottom of a baking pan with half of the oil.

2.   Rub the chicken pieces with the remaining oil and the garlic halves, then sprinkle the rosemary and salt and pepper over each piece. Arrange the chicken, skin side up, in the pan and bake uncovered for about 50 minutes, or until done. Baste the chicken with the white wine throughout the baking period.

3.   While the chicken is cooking prepare the sauce and vegetables. Combine the Espagnole Sauce, stock, vinegar, dry mustard, salt and pepper in a saucepan. Bring to a boil and simmer for 5 minutes.

4.   Melt the butter in a skillet and sauté the mushrooms until they are tender.

5.   Blanch the carrots and pearl onions in salted boiling water. Drain and add to the mushrooms. Stir to mix. Set aside.

6.   After the chicken has cooked for 40 minutes, baste it with ¼ cup of the sauce. When the chicken is done, degrease the pan juices and strain them into the remaining sauce. Simmer for 3 minutes.

7.   Heat the vegetables over moderate heat for 2 to 3 minutes.

8.   Arrange the chicken on a warm serving platter and arrange the vegetables around it. Pour the sauce over the chicken and vegetables and serve immediately.

Petto di Pollo con Broccoli
Stuffed Chicken Breast with Broccoli
and Pesto Cream Sauce
Serves 4

2	cups broccoli flowerets, blanched	4	teaspoons plus 2 tablespoons Pesto (page 119)
1	cup chopped fresh mushrooms		Freshly ground black pepper, and salt
½	cup chopped mozzarella	4	thin slices of prosciutto
¼	cup freshly grated Parmigiano	½	cup clarified butter (page 309)
½	cup bread crumbs	¼	cup dry white wine
1	teaspoon dried rosemary or chopped fresh rosemary leaves	¼	cup chicken stock (page 65)
		1	cup light cream
4	large chicken breasts, boned but not skinned	2	tablespoons dry sherry

1.   In a food processor, blend together the broccoli, mushrooms, mozzarella, Parmigiano, bread crumbs and rosemary. Do not over-blend as it will become pasty. Set aside.

2.   Lay the breasts between two sheets of wax paper and pound them lightly. Lay the flattened breasts skin side down on a work surface. Spread 1 teaspoon of Pesto on each breast and sprinkle with a little pepper. Place one fourth of the stuffing in the center of each and top with a slice of prosciutto. Roll the chicken around the stuffing and secure with a toothpick.

3.   Heat the butter in a skillet and brown the breasts on all sides. Add the wine and stock, cover, and simmer for 7 minutes. Remove the breasts from the pan and keep them warm. Simmer the sauce for 5 minutes more, then set aside.

4.   In another skillet, heat the cream. Add the remaining 2 tablespoons of Pesto, the sherry and the sauce to the cream, whisking constantly. Simmer for 3 minutes or until the sauce is slightly thickened.

5.   Remove the toothpicks from the chicken and cut the breasts into ½-inch-thick slices. To do this, place the stuffed breast, seam side down, on a cutting board. Using a sharp knife, slice from top to bottom slightly on the diagonal. The stuffing will remain intact and you will have a circle of white chicken meat around the colorful stuffing. You should have about 5 round slices. Arrange these on the plate by overlapping the slices slightly. Pour the cream sauce over the chicken slices and serve immediately.

Pollo al Bergamo
Chicken Breast Stuffed with Sausage
Serves 4

4	large chicken breasts, boned, but not skinned	1	tablespoon garlic, finely chopped
6	Italian sweet sausages, cooked, skinned and coarsely chopped		Salt and freshly ground black pepper
¾	cup thinly sliced fresh mushrooms	⅓	cup clarified butter (page 309)
¼	cup slivered blanched almonds	2	tablespoons olive oil
1½	tablespoons dried basil	2	garlic cloves
2	teaspoons dried fennel seeds, crushed	½	cup dry white wine
		1	cup Balsamella (page 267)
		1	tablespoon finely chopped Fresh parsley or basil

1.   Lay the breasts between two sheets of wax paper and pound them lightly. Lay the flattened breasts skin side down on a work surface. In the center of each fillet place one fourth each of the sausage meat, mushrooms and almonds, and a sprinkle of the basil, fennel, garlic, salt and pepper. Fold the chicken over the stuffing and pin together with a toothpick.
2.   Heat the butter and oil in a large skillet. Add the garlic cloves and sauté until golden, then remove and discard. Add the stuffed chicken breasts and brown them on all sides. Add the wine and cook for another 10 minutes, turning the breasts continually (be careful not to tear the skin).
3.   Transfer the cooked breasts to a cutting board. Remove the toothpicks and slice each breast as for the Petto di Pollo con Broccoli recipe. Lay the slices on a warm serving dish and pour the Balsamella, which should be hot, along the center of the rounds. Garnish with parsley or fresh basil leaves and serve immediately.

Pollo in Padella
Chicken Breast Stuffed with Mushrooms and Herbs
Serves 4

4	large chicken breasts, boned but not skinned	¼	teaspoon chopped fresh thyme leaves or dried thyme
4	thin slices mozzarella	½	cup clarified butter (page 309)
½	cup thinly sliced fresh mushrooms	¼	cup olive oil
		¾	cup dry white wine
1½	cups bread crumbs	1	tablespoon lemon juice
⅔	cup freshly grated Parmigiano	1	large egg
2	tablespoons finely chopped fresh parsley leaves		Dash of Tabasco sauce
			Salt and freshly ground black pepper
1	tablespoon dried basil		
1½	teaspoons finely chopped garlic	4	thin slices prosciutto
		½	cup chicken stock (page 65)

1.   Lay the breasts between 2 sheets of wax paper and pound them lightly. Lay the flattened breasts skin side down on a work surface. Place 1 slice of mozzarella and 4 or 5 mushroom slices on each breast.

2.   Make the stuffing: In a mixing bowl, combine the bread crumbs, grated cheese, parsley, basil, ½ teaspoon of the garlic, thyme, ¼ cup of the butter, 2 tablespoons of the olive oil, ¼ cup of the wine, lemon juice, egg, Tabasco sauce and salt and pepper to taste.

3.   Place 3 or 4 tablespoons of the stuffing in the center of each breast and cover the stuffing with a slice of prosciutto. Roll the chicken over the stuffing and secure with a toothpick.

4.   Heat the remaining butter and oil in a skillet and brown the rolled breasts on all sides. Lower the heat and add the remaining wine and garlic. Season with salt and pepper and simmer for 7 minutes.

5.   Remove the breasts from the pan and put them on a warm plate and

keep warm. Add the chicken stock to the juices in the pan and simmer for 3 minutes. Season with salt and pepper, if necessary.

6.   Remove the toothpicks from the breasts and slice the chicken as for the Petto di Pollo con Broccoli recipe. Arrange the slices on a warm serving dish and pour the sauce over them. Serve immediately.

Pollo al Casimello
Sautéed Chicken with Prosciutto and Madeira
Serves 4

4	whole chicken breasts, boned and skinned	½	teaspoon dried savory freshly ground black pepper
½	cup clarified butter (page 309)	10	thin slices mozzarella, chopped
10	thin slices prosciutto, diced	4	tablespoons finely chopped fresh parsley leaves
4	garlic cloves, pressed		
½	cup dry Madeira		
½	cup Espagnole Sauce (page 271)		

1.   Cut the breasts in half. Then cut each piece in half on the bias. Lay the pieces between two sheets of wax paper and pound until very thin.

2.   Heat the butter in a large skillet and sauté the prosciutto lightly. Add the chicken and garlic and brown the chicken on both sides. Transfer the chicken to a warm plate.

3.   Add the Madeira, Espagnole sauce, savory and pepper to the pan. Simmer for 3 minutes. Return the chicken to the pan and simmer for a minute on each side. Sprinkle the mozzarella over the chicken. Cover the pan and cook just until the cheese has melted. Sprinkle with the parsley and serve at once.

Pollo con Funghi e Finocchio
Chicken with Mushrooms and Fennel
Serves 6

1	large bulb fennel, sliced ¼-inch thick	1	cup dry vermouth
4	tablespoons canola or olive oil	4	cups quartered mushrooms
1	3½-pound fryer chicken, cut in pieces	2	tablespoons capers
1	cup chopped scallions	1	tablespoon Dijon mustard
		1	tablespoon crushed rosemary

1.   Blanch fennel, drain and set aside.

2.   Heat 2 tablespoons oil in a skillet. Add chicken and cook uncovered over moderate heat, turning often. When chicken is browned, remove and set aside.

3.   Drain fat, add 2 tablespoons oil and the chopped scallions and cook until wilted. Add vermouth and reduce by half. Add mushrooms, capers, mustard, and rosemary. Simmer on low heat 5 minutes, then add fennel. Return chicken to pan and heat through.

NOTE: Fennel has a flavor much like licorice. Combined with other flavors, it adds an unusual, subtle note.

Pollo alla Genovese
Chicken with Herbs and Vegetables
Serves 4

4	chicken breasts, boned but not skinned	4	teaspoons butter
	Fresh rosemary leaves	1	carrot, finely chopped
	Fresh basil leaves	1	celery stalk, finely chopped
	Ground nutmeg	1	large onion, finely chopped
	Finely chopped garlic	⅔	cup clarified butter (page 309)
	Finely chopped fresh sage	½	cup dry white wine
	Fresh tarragon leaves	¼	cup chicken stock (page 65)
	Fresh thyme leaves	8	lengthwise slices of eggplant, ¼-inch-thick
4	tablespoons freshly grated Parmigiano	8	artichoke hearts, lightly steamed
4	teaspoons finely chopped fresh parsley leaves	¼	lemon
12	fresh mushrooms, stem ends trimmed		Salt and freshly ground black pepper

1.   Lay the breasts between two sheets of wax paper and pound them lightly. Lay the flattened breasts skin side down on a work surface. Sprinkle each with a pinch of all the herbs. In the center, put 1 tablespoon of the Parmigiano, 1 teaspoon of the parsley, 2 or 3 whole mushrooms and 1 teaspoon of butter. Roll the chicken over the filling and secure with 2 toothpicks.

2.   Heat 6 tablespoons of the clarified butter in a skillet. Add the breasts and brown them on all sides. Lower the heat and add the carrot, celery, onion, wine and stock. Cook for 10 minutes. Add the artichoke hearts and cook for 5 minutes more. Strain the sauce from the pan and set it aside. Keep the sauce and chicken warm.

3.   Lay the eggplant strips on a buttered baking sheet, brush their tops with clarified butter and broil until light brown. Arrange the eggplant on a warm serving dish.

4.   Remove the toothpicks from the chicken and slice each breast as for the Petto di Pollo con Broccoli recipe. Lay the slices over the eggplant. Arrange the artichoke hearts and the chopped vegetables around the chicken. Pour the sauce over both the chicken and the vegetables and serve immediately.

Pollo alla Zingarella
Chicken with Piquant Sauce
Serves 4

4	8-ounce chicken breasts, boned and skinned	½	cup white wine vinegar
	Salt and freshly ground black pepper	2	tablespoons capers, rinsed, drained and finely chopped
2	tablespoons olive oil	8	anchovy fillets, rinsed, dried and finely chopped
2	tablespoons butter	4	small pickled onions, chopped
½	cup chopped scallions (white and tender green parts)	½	garlic clove, finely chopped
2	tablespoons all-purpose flour	3	tablespoons finely chopped fresh parsley leaves
1	small garlic clove, crushed		
½	cup dry white wine		
2	tablespoons tomato paste (diluted with 4 tablespoons of the wine)		

1.   Lay the breasts between 2 sheets of wax paper and pound them lightly. Season them with salt and pepper.

2.   Heat the oil and butter in a skillet. Add the scallions and sauté until they soften. Add the breasts and brown them on both sides, then sprinkle them with the flour. Add the garlic and wine and let the wine reduce by half, then add the diluted tomato paste, salt and pepper.

3.   Lower the heat and cook for 5 minutes. Remove the breasts from the pan and keep them warm. Continue to cook the pan juices over low heat for 10 minutes.

4.   While that is cooking, make the second part of your sauce in another pan: Simmer the wine vinegar until it is reduced slightly. Add the remaining ingredients and simmer for another 2 minutes.

5.   Return the chicken to the original skillet. Pour the sauce from the second pan over the chicken. Stir gently, to mix the two sauces.

6.   Arrange the chicken on a warm serving plate, and pour the sauce over the breasts. Serve immediately.

Pollo con Senape
Grilled Chicken with Mustard
Serves 4

2½	teaspoons Dijon mustard	1	3 to 4 pound chicken, split
1	clove garlic	1	lemon, juice of
2	tablespoons balsamic vinegar	1	lemon, sliced
2	tablespoons minced fresh basil	2	large sprigs of fresh rosemary
	Salt and pepper		

1.   Mix all ingredients except lemon. Place chicken skin side down and brush with marinade. Broil for 10 minutes, turn and baste. Keep basting and turning. When juices run clear, approximately 35 minutes, chicken is cooked.

2.   Add lemon juice to defatted pan juices. Garnish with lemon slices and fresh rosemary.

Pollo con Rabe
Chicken with Broccoli Rabe
Serves 2

1	tablespoon olive oil	2	small bunches of broccoli rabe, trimmed
2	tablespoons shallots, finely chopped	1	teaspoon dry mustard
2	whole scallions, coarsely chopped		Salt and pepper
2	chicken breasts, skinned and pounded	1	tablespoon dehydrated potato (instant mashed)
1½	cups dry vermouth or white wine		Parsley for garnish

1. Heat oil in a sauté pan, add shallots and scallions. When glazed add breasts which have been rubbed with pepper and mustard. Cook each side for 2 minutes.
2. Add heated wine and simmer for 5 minutes. Add broccoli rabe and cook for 6 minutes. Season with salt and pepper.
3. When breasts are firm to the touch, remove from heat. Place rabe on a heated platter, cover with chicken breasts.
4. Add dehydrated potato to liquid, bring to boil. Reduce heat. When creamy, spoon over chicken. Garnish with Italian parsley.

Pollo alla Fiorentina
Sautéed Chicken Breast with Mushrooms and Spinach
Serves 6

6	whole chicken breasts, boned but not skinned	1	pound fresh spinach, tough stems removed
6	small shallots, finely chopped	8	tablespoons butter
6	scallions (white and tender green parts), thinly sliced	1	cup thinly sliced domestic mushrooms
	Freshly ground nutmeg	1	cup heavy cream
2	cups dry white wine		Salt and freshly ground white
5	cups chicken stock		pepper

1.   Lay the chicken breasts between two sheets of wax paper and pound them lightly. Season the skinless side with salt, pepper and nutmeg. Sprinkle each breast with the shallots and scallions. Fold each breast into an envelope shape (they should be as large as possible).

2.   Combine the wine and stock in a pan and heat slowly. Poach the breasts, seam side down, in the wine and stock until done (about 10 to 15 minutes). Remove the breasts from the pan and keep them warm. Strain the poaching liquid into a new pan. Bring the liquid to a boil and let it reduce by half.

3.   While this is reducing, prepare the vegetables. Heat the butter in a skillet and sauté the mushrooms until tender. Season with salt and pepper, remove the mushrooms from the pan and add the spinach (if necessary, add more butter to the pan before adding the spinach). Sauté the spinach just until tender and season with salt, pepper and nutmeg. Arrange the spinach over the bottom of a warm serving plate. Sprinkle the mushrooms over the spinach.

4.   Now add the cream to the reduced stock-wine sauce. Season with salt and pepper and simmer for 3 minutes.

5.   Arrange the chicken breasts, either whole or sliced, on the bed of vegetables. Pour the sauce over all.

Fegatini di Pollo
Chicken Livers Sautéed with White Wine and Basil
Serves 4

½ cup clarified butter (page 309)
2 pounds chicken livers,
cleaned and cut into halves
½ lemon
6 tablespoons dry white wine
1 teaspoon dried basil or
Chopped fresh basil leaves

Salt and freshly ground black
pepper
4 tablespoons finely chopped
fresh parsley leaves

1. Heat the butter in a large skillet and brown the livers over a high flame. Squeeze the lemon juice into the pan, add the remaining ingredients and cook for 2 to 3 minutes. If you desire them well done, reduce the heat and continue cooking.
2. The fegatini may also be made with mushrooms. Simply add a handful of sliced mushrooms to the livers at the beginning of the cooking.
3. Either fegatini preparation is excellent served with spaghetti. Cook the spaghetti in salted boiling water until al dente. Drain it and transfer it to a warm serving bowl. Pour the fegatini and its sauce over the spaghetti and toss lightly.

Fegatini di Pollo con Salvia
Sautéed Chicken Livers with Sage and Prosciutto
Serves 4

2   tablespoons butter

1   cup bread crumbs

1   teaspoon finely chopped garlic

1   teaspoon dried basil

1   teaspoon finely chopped fresh parsley leaves

Salt and freshly ground black pepper

6   tablespoons clarified butter (page 309)

6   thin slices prosciutto, chopped

2   pounds chicken livers, cleaned and cut into halves

2   garlic cloves, finely chopped

1   teaspoon dried thyme

4   leaves fresh sage, chopped

6   tablespoons Marsala

½   lemon

4   thin slices prosciutto

2   tablespoons freshly grated Parmigiano

1.   Preheat the broiler.

2.   Melt the butter in a skillet, then add the bread crumbs, 1 teaspoon garlic, basil, parsley and salt and pepper to taste. Toast the crumbs until golden and set them aside.

3.   Heat the clarified butter in another skillet and brown the chopped prosciutto lightly. Add the livers, garlic, thyme, sage, pepper and Marsala. Cook for 1 minute. Squeeze the lemon juice into the pan.

4.   Transfer the livers and sauce to an oven-proof dish. Lay the slices of prosciutto over the livers and sprinkle with the seasoned bread crumbs and Parmigiano. Broil until the crumbs are browned. Serve immediately.

CARNE
Meat

Maiale nel Fuoco alla Genovina
Genovina's Pork Cooked Over the Fire

This method of cooking not only pork, but also beef, veal, chicken and salt cod (pre-soaked) was taught to me by a dear friend in Capodimonte, a small lakeside town north of Rome. As the cool weather arrived she would light a fire in the fireplace, and on a small grating which she placed over the hot embers, she would cook all of the above foods as well as slices of her homemade pecorino cheese.

1.   Heat your grill or broiler. The meat or chicken should be cut into individual portions (chops work very well). Rub salt and pepper into the meat. If desired, crushed fennel seed may also be rubbed into the meat.

2.   Pour some olive oil onto a plate. Cut a clove of garlic in half and add it to the oil. Take a long, full sprig of fresh rosemary and coat it in the oil.

3.   Place the meat on the grill. As it is cooking, baste it with the rosemary dipped in the oil. (Dip the sprig in the oil and pass it lightly over the meat.) Turn the meat once and cook to desired doneness.

Petto di Vitello
Grilled and Braised Veal Breast
Serves 4 to 6

2	tablespoon olive oil		1	teaspoon dry thyme
3	large onions, chopped		1	12-ounce can beer
1	4-pound bone-in veal breast			Salt and pepper
3	cloves garlic, minced			

1.   In an oven-proof casserole heat 1 tablespoon oil, sauté the onions until wilted, then remove. Add another tablespoon oil, sear the veal breast, and remove.

2.   Return onions to pan, place meat on top, add remaining ingredients and bring to a boil. Bake in 375-degree oven for 1½ hours or until tender, basting frequently. Slice veal and serve with pan juices over linguini.

Costolette di Vitello alla Madeira
Grilled Stuffed Veal Chop in Madeira Sauce
Serves 4

4	veal chops, with pocket		Salt and pepper	
1	teaspoon canola or olive oil			

STUFFING

4	slices lean prosciutto, minced	2	teaspoons grated lemon peel	
½	cup finely chopped red onion	2	tablespoons chopped parsley	
1	tablespoon minced fresh sage	2	tablespoons Espagnol sauce	
1	tablespoon minced fresh chervil		(page 271)	
		2	tablespoons olive oil	
		1	cup fresh bread crumbs	

Combine all of the above.

SAUCE

4	tablespoons veal stock			
	Juice of ½ lemon		fresh ground black pepper	
2	tablespoons capers	½	cup diced shallots	
		¾	cup Madeira wine	

Combine and simmer all ingredient until reduced by half.

1.   Trim chops and season with salt and pepper. Fill pockets with stuffing mixture.

2.   Rub chops with a little oil and place under preheated broiler for about 2 minutes each side. Turn oven to 300 degrees and open oven door for 1 minute to bring down temperature, then close door. Bake chops for 30 minutes.

3.   Place two tablespoon sauce on each preheated platter and set chop on top. Garnish with fresh sage.

Cosciotto di Vitello
Roast Leg of Veal with Fennel and Cream
Servings will depend on size of veal leg

1	veal leg, bone in		1	bulb fresh fennel
	2 teaspoons butter			cut into large pieces
	Freshly ground black pepper		1	tablespoon dried basil
	A handful of fresh sage			Salt
	leaves		3	cups (approximately) veal
½	pound pancetta			stock
2	large carrots, peeled and cut		1	cup (approximately) dry
	into large chunks			white wine
1	large onion, cut into large		1	cup heavy cream
	pieces		1	cup buttermilk, sour cream
				or creme fraîche

1.   Preheat the oven to 425 degrees.

2.   Trim the fat from the leg and dress it. Rub butter and black pepper over the entire leg. Slice a pocket in the leg and stuff it with the sage.

3.   In a large heavy skillet, cook the pancetta over moderate heat until it gives up its fat (this is called "rendering"). Remove the pieces of meat, add the veal to the skillet and brown it on all sides in the fat.

4.   Place the leg on a rack in a roasting pan. Surround it with the vegetables. Sprinkle the basil, salt and pepper over the vegetables and roast for 15 minutes. Lower the oven temperature to 325 degrees and continue to roast, allowing 15 minutes per pound. Baste with the veal stock and wine throughout the roasting period.

5.   Remove the veal from the pan and cover it to keep it warm while you prepare the sauce.

6.   Place the roasting pan on your stove burners and bring the juices in the pan to a boil. Scrape the sides and bottom of the pan and mix these particles in with the juices. Let boil for 2 minutes. Strain the juices

through cheesecloth into a heavy saucepan and bring them to a boil.

7.   Whisk in the cream and stir over moderate heat for 2 minutes. Whisk in the buttermilk, sour cream or creme fraîche. Allow the sauce to reduce by half.

8.   Slice the leg. To do so, hold the leg by the shank and slice down and around. Make the slices 6 or 7 inches long and ¼-inch thick. Slices should not exceed 3 inches across. Overlap the slices on a hot plate and pour some of the sauce over the meat. Serve immediately.

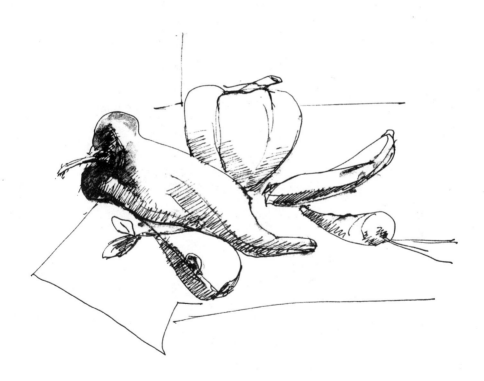

Arrosto di Vitello
Roasted Loin of Veal Stuffed with Prosciutto and Watercress
Serves 10 to 12

2	cups fresh bread crumbs	1	8- to 9-pound veal loin
	Milk		(weight with bone in)
2	pounds Italian sweet sausage,	12	thin slices prosciutto
	removed from the casing and	1	bunch watercress, all thick
	puréed in a blender		stems removed
1	pound veal, ground and	1	cup olive oil
	then puréed in a blender		Caul fat or thinly sliced pork
1	chicken breast, ground and		fat, enough to wrap around
	puréed in a blender		the loin
3	fresh eggs, lightly beaten	2	onions, coarsely chopped
10	sage leaves, chopped	2	celery stalks, coarsely chopped
2	tablespoons finely chopped	1	bunch carrots, finely chopped
	fresh parsley leaves	8	cups dry white wine
	Salt and freshly ground black	8	cups veal stock
	pepper	6	sage leaves

1.   Preheat the oven to 300 degrees.

2.   To make the forcemeat, combine the bread crumbs and enough milk to cover in a large bowl. Allow the bread to absorb all the milk. Add the sausage, veal, chicken, eggs, sage and parsley to the softened bread crumbs. Season with a generous amount of salt and pepper. Mix thoroughly and set aside.

3.   Butterfly the veal loin or have the butcher do it for you, and lay it out flat. Season the inside of the loin with salt and pepper. Lay six slices of prosciutto over half the loin. Form the forcemeat into a loaf shape and

place it on the prosciutto (see note). Now lay the watercress down the center of the loaf and cover with the remaining 6 slices of prosciutto. Fold the other half of the loin over the forcemeat and roll the loin so that it fits snugly around the forcemeat. Sew the seams together. Tie the loin securely and then rub the outside with salt and pepper.

4.   Heat the oil or fat in a large pan and brown the veal on all sides. If using sliced pork fat, blanch it before wrapping it around the loin. Otherwise, wrap the caul fat securely around the loin and tie it once again.

5.   Spread the onions, celery and carrots over the bottom of a roasting pan and lay the loin on top. Add the wine and stock to the pan and roast for 45 minutes, basting occasionally.

6.   Remove the veal from the pan and place it in a warm spot. Strain the vegetables from the pan and purée them. Combine the purée with the remaining pan juices in a saucepan and heat slowly. If the sauce is too thick, add more veal stock. Season with the sage leaves and more salt and pepper. Simmer for 5 minutes. Serve the sauce with the sliced veal.

NOTE: Extra forcemeat may be shaped into small loaves and cooked with the roast. This forcemeat is delightful served with fettuccine that has been tossed in the sauce from the roast.

Costolette di Vitello in Padella
Veal Chops Cooked in a Pan
Serves 2

2	veal chops, 12 to 14 ounces each	4	ounces fontina cheese, sliced
1	tablespoon olive oil	2	tablespoons Dijon mustard
3	cloves garlic, minced	1	tablespoon balsamic vinegar
1	12-ounce can of Italian plum tomatoes, chopped	1	tablespoon white vinegar
8	basil leaves	4	medium potatoes, peeled, sliced and cooked
		2	cups broccoli spears, parboiled

1.   In a heavy skillet, brown chops in the oil. Remove chops, add garlic and cook on medium heat for 2 minutes.

2.   Add tomatoes and basil and simmer 15 minutes. Return chops to pan, top with fontina, cover and simmer on low for 10 minutes or just until chops are firm to touch.

3.   Combine mustard and vinegars. Toss with potatoes and broccoli, season with salt and pepper and heat through. Serve with chops.

Vitello alla Sforza
Broiled Veal Chop with Espagnole Sauce
Serves 4

4	10-ounce veal chops, pounded lightly	½	cup clarified butter (page 309)
	Salt and freshly ground black pepper		Juice of one lemon
		1⅓	cup Espagnole Sauce (page 271)

1.   Preheat the broiler.

2.   Rub salt and pepper into each veal chop. Combine the butter and lemon juice in an oven-proof baking pan. Add the chops to the pan and turn to coat the chops with the butter.

3.   Broil the chops on each side until they are firm to the touch. Just before they are done, drain the fat from the pan and add the Espagnole Sauce. Cook just until the chops are done and the sauce is warm.

Vitello al Forno
Veal Top Split and Roasted
Serves 6 to 8

1	3-pound prime veal top of the round	2	stems fresh marjoram or ½ teaspoon dry	
6	slices pancetta	1	tablespoon chopped parsley	
½	cup porcini mushrooms, soaked in water to cover	1	tablespoon olive oil	
¼	cup slivered almonds	1	tablespoon butter	
4	sprigs fresh rosemary or 1 teaspoon dry	1	cup dry white wine	
			Salt and pepper	

1. Lay open the veal, rub pocket with salt and pepper and line with pancetta. Add herbs, almonds and mushrooms and tie veal with cotton twine.

2. Combine the mushroom water with the wine and reserve.

3. Brown veal in a heavy casserole in a little olive oil and butter. Roast in a 350-degree oven for 50 to 60 minutes or just until juices run clear, basting frequently with wine mixture.

NOTE: Veal has very little fat in the meat. Always take care not to overcook it or it will become dry.

Osso Buco
Braised Veal Shank in Espagnole Sauce
Serves 4

½	cup all-purpose flour	1	onion, finely chopped
	Salt and freshly ground black pepper	1	garlic clove, finely chopped
		½	cup dry white wine
4	veal shanks, 2 inches in diameter and tied with a string across the middle (This keeps the meat around the bone.)	1	bay leaf
		½	cup Espagnole Sauce (page 271)
		½	cup veal stock (page 64)
		2	cups Italian peeled plum tomatoes, drained, seeded and chopped
¼	cup olive oil		
¼	cup clarified butter (page 309)		
2	carrots, cut into small dice	2	tablespoons finely chopped fresh parsley leaves
1	celery stalk, cut into small dice	1	recipe of Risotto alla Milanese (page 124)

1.   Preheat the oven to 325 degrees.

2.   Season the flour with a little salt and pepper. Dredge the shanks in the flour, then shake to remove any excess.

3.   Heat the oil in a skillet and brown the shanks well on all sides. Drain on paper towels.

4.   Heat the butter in another skillet and add the carrots, celery, onion and garlic. Sauté for 5 minutes. Add the wine and bay leaf and cook for 5 minutes more.

5.   In a baking pan just large enough to hold the shanks, spread the vegetable mixture over the bottom of the pan. Lay the veal shanks over the vegetables and add the Espagnole Sauce, stock, tomatoes and parsley. Bake, uncovered, for 2½ hours, turning and basting the veal every 30 minutes.

6.   Remove the string from the shanks, being careful to keep the meat around the bone. Spread the Risotto Milanese over a warm serving platter. Arrange the shanks in the center of the rice and pour the sauce from the baking pan over all.

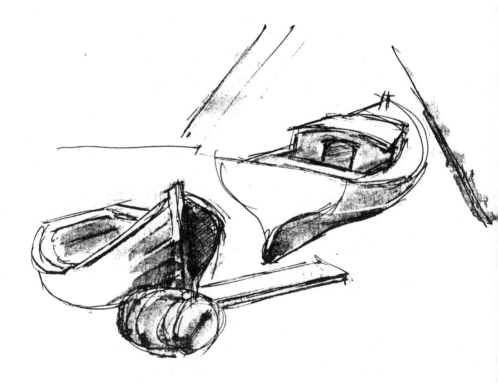

Vitello alla Filomena
Marinated Veal Baked with Eggplant and Tomatoes
Serves 6

2	cups red wine vinegar	1	tablespoon finely chopped garlic
2	cups water		
1	cup extra virgin olive oil	½	cup clarified butter (page 309)
2	garlic cloves, crushed	2	eggplants (about 1½ pounds each)
1	onion, finely chopped		
1	tablespoon dried basil	1½	cups Espagnole Sauce (page 271)
1	bay leaf		
½	teaspoon freshly ground black pepper	1½	cups freshly grated Parmigiano
3	pounds boneless veal, trimmed and cut into 1-inch cubes	3	cups Italian plum tomatoes, drained, seeded and diced
			Salt and freshly ground black pepper
¾	cup olive oil		

1. Start marinade 3 to 4 days in advance.
2. Combine the first 8 ingredients in a bowl. Add the veal cubes, cover and marinate in the refrigerator for 3 or 4 days. Stir every 12 hours. Drain well before using.
3. Preheat the oven to 375 degrees.
4. Heat ½ cup of the olive oil in a skillet. Add the garlic and veal and brown the veal cubes on all sides. Remove them from the pan and drain them on paper towels. Set them aside.
5. Cut the ends off the eggplants and then cut each eggplant in half lengthwise. Lay them cut side down and cut them along their lengths into ¼-inch slices. Discard the end slices. Brush each slice with a little of the clarified butter and lay them on a baking sheet. Bake the eggplant slices until they are light brown. Drain the eggplant on paper towels. Do not turn

off the oven.

6.   Combine the veal and Espagnole Sauce in a bowl and toss to coat the cubes. Drain the sauce from the bowl and reserve.

7.   Grease the bottom of a 9- by 13- by 2-inch roasting pan with the remaining oil and butter. Cover the bottom of the pan with eggplant slices. Sprinkle the eggplant with a little salt, pepper and Parmigiano. Spread one third of the tomatoes over the eggplant and sprinkle some of the basil on the tomatoes. Cover the tomatoes with a layer of veal cubes. Cover the veal with a layer of eggplant and repeat the process. The last layer should be tomatoes. (Be sure to reserve ½ cup of the Parmigiano for the topping.) Pour the reserved Espagnole Sauce over the tomatoes and top with the remaining Parmigiano. (This process may also be done in individual ceramic baking dishes.)

8.   Cover the pan with aluminum foil and bake for 35 minutes.

Scaloppini con Senape
Sautéed Veal in Mustard Sauce
Serves 4

1¼   pounds boneless veal, top
round or rump
¼   cup clarified butter (page 309)
1   cup thinly sliced mushrooms
½   teaspoon dried basil
¼   teaspoon dried thyme
2   tablespoons brandy

¼   cup dry red wine
1   tablespoon Dijon mustard
1   tablespoon capers, rinsed and
drained
Salt and freshly ground black
pepper

1.   Cutting across the grain, slice the veal into ¼-inch-thick wafers. Pound the veal gently between sheets of wax paper.

2.   Heat the butter in a skillet and sauté the veal until lightly browned on both sides. Add the mushrooms, basil, thyme and half of the brandy. Let the brandy burn off, then add the red wine and cook for 1 minute. Remove the veal to a warm serving plate.

3.   Stir the mustard into the sauce. Add the remaining brandy, capers, salt and pepper. Reduce until slightly thickened. Spoon the mushrooms and sauce over the veal and serve immediately.

Vitello alla Milanese
Breaded Veal Sautéed with Garlic and Lemon
Serves 4

2	large eggs, beaten	4	7-ounce veal cutlets, cut ¼ inch thick
2	tablespoons milk		
	Salt and freshly ground black pepper	½	cup olive oil
1	cup bread crumbs	1	teaspoon finely chopped garlic
		4	lemon wedges

1.   Beat the eggs and milk together in a shallow pan. Season with salt and pepper and set aside.

2.   Place the bread crumbs in another shallow pan and season with salt and pepper. Set aside.

3.   Lay the veal cutlets between sheets of wax paper and pound until very thin. Dip each cutlet in the egg wash (let any excess egg drip off) and then coat the cutlets with the bread crumbs, pressing lightly with your hand to make sure the crumbs adhere to the meat. Shake off any excess crumbs. Refrigerate for 2 hours before cooking.

4.   Heat the oil in a large skillet over moderate heat. Add the cutlets and the garlic and sauté until golden on each side.

5.   Transfer the cutlets to paper towels to drain. Serve immediately on a warm platter with the lemon wedges.

Vitello alla Parmigiana
Veal with Parmigiano and Ragù
Serves 4

4   7-ounce veal cutlets, breaded
and fried as for Vitello alla
Milanese (page 205)

1½ cups Ragù (page 117), heated

4   tablespoons freshly grated
Parmigiano

12   thin (1- by 3-inch) slices of
mozzarella

1.   Preheat the broiler.
2.   Arrange the cutlets on an oven-proof platter. Cover each with the
Ragù, but do not flood the cutlets in the sauce. Sprinkle each cutlet with 1
tablespoon of the Parmigiano, then place 3 slices of the mozzarella on
each.
3.   Broil just until the cheese melts.

Saltimbocca alla Romana
Veal Rolls Stuffed with Prosciutto and Mozzarella
Serves 6

12	thin slices veal, pounded	6	tablespoons clarified butter
12	thin slices prosciutto		(page 309)
12	thin slices mozzarella	½	cup dry white wine
3	tablespoons dried basil or	6	teaspoons fresh lemon juice
	chopped fresh basil leaves	2	teaspoons finely chopped fresh
2	teaspoons chopped fresh sage		parsley leaves
	leaves		Salt and freshly ground black
	Freshly ground black pepper		pepper
4	tablespoons cream sherry	6	lemon wedges for garnish

1.   Lay the slices of veal on a work surface. Place a slice of prosciutto and a slice of mozzarella on each. Sprinkle with a little of the basil, sage and black pepper. Roll up the veal tightly into cylinders and fasten with a toothpick.

2.   Heat a skillet over high heat and pour the sherry into the hot pan, tipping the pan to coat the bottom evenly. Add the butter and, when it is hot, brown the veal rolls completely. Add the white wine, lemon juice and parsley to the pan and season with salt and pepper. Lower the heat and cook for 10 to 15 minutes.

3.   Transfer the veal rolls to a warm serving dish and garnish with lemon wedges.

Vitello Piccato
Sautéed Veal with Mushrooms and Cream
Serves 4

½   cup clarified butter (page 309)
20   ounces veal wafers (see recipe
      for Scaloppine alla Marsala,
      page 212)
1   cup thinly sliced fresh
      mushrooms
1   teaspoon finely chopped garlic
2   teaspoons fresh lemon juice

Salt and freshly ground black
      pepper
½   cup dry white wine
1   cup veal stock (page 64)
      Juice of 1 lemon
1   cup heavy cream

1.   Heat the butter in a large skillet. Add the veal, mushrooms and ½
teaspoon of the garlic, and brown the veal lightly on both sides. Add the
lemon juice and salt and pepper. Transfer the veal and mushrooms to a
warm serving platter and keep them warm while you make the sauce.
2.   Add the wine to the pan and bring it to a boil over high heat.
Continue boiling it for 1 minute. Add the veal stock, lemon juice, remaining garlic and salt and pepper to taste. Boil for 3 to 4 minutes. Add the
heavy cream and simmer for another 4 minutes, or until the sauce is slightly thickened. Add more salt and pepper if necessary. Pour this sauce over
the veal and mushrooms and serve immediately.

Medaglioni di Vitello
Sautéed Medallions of Veal in Brandy-Butter Sauce
Serves 4

1	cup all-purpose flour	6	tablespoons clarified butter (page 309)
	Salt and freshly ground black pepper	4	tablespoons brandy
24	ounces veal, cut into ⅜-inch-thick medallions	6	tablespoons Espagnole Sauce (page 271)
		2	tablespoons butter, softened

1.   Season the flour with a pinch of salt and pepper. Dredge the medallions in the flour and shake off any excess.

2.   Heat the clarified butter in a skillet. Add the medallions and brown on both sides. Add the brandy and Espagnole Sauce and cook for about 5 minutes over medium heat.

3.   Transfer the veal to a warm serving platter and keep it warm. Over high heat, add salt and pepper to taste, and whisk the butter quickly into the sauce. Pour the sauce over the medallions and serve immediately.

*R*estaurant reviewers and patrons of Ciro and Sal's have described as "romantic" the murky brick cellar on Kiley Court that is the main room of the restaurant. Ciro has many memories of famous people who have enjoyed the restaurant's funky Bohemian ambiance.

The patronage of celebrities has not gone to his head, however. On the contrary, he delights in telling stories in which he is the butt of the joke. One of his favorites took place many years ago, the night the hostess whispered to him that Edward G. Robinson, the actor renowned for his portrayal of gangsters, had arrived, unannounced, at the reception desk.

Ciro and the staff were thrilled and everyone peered furtively to catch a glimpse of the man. The Star was splendid in his navy blue blazer with bright brass buttons, red silk ascot and pale cream summer-weight gabardine slacks, which Ciro refers to as "ice cream pants." A study in impeccable taste, the actor peered inquiringly into the funky darkness of the cellar, with the Chianti bottles holding dripping candles, rusty cheese graters that served as lampshades and nail kegs that did duty as chairs. Mr. Robinson looked down at his immaculate white pants, shook his head and abruptly departed without a word.

Noce di Vitello alla Bolognese
Veal and Chicken Livers Sautéed
with Prosciutto and Esrom
Serves 4

1⅓   cups cream sherry
¾   cup water
2   garlic cloves, finely chopped
     Freshly ground black pepper
1   pound veal, thinly sliced
¾   cup clarified butter (page 309)
6   chicken livers, cleaned and
     coarsely chopped
1   teaspoon dried basil
     Pinch of dried thyme
2   garlic cloves, finely chopped

     Salt and freshly ground black
     pepper
6   thin slices prosciutto,
     trimmed of excess fat
6   thin (1½- by 3-inch) slices
     of mozzarella
6   thin (1½- by 3-inch) slices
     of esrom
4   tablespoons dry white wine
2   tablespoons finely chopped
     fresh parsley leaves

1.   Start the marinade the day before.
2.   Combine the first 4 ingredients in a bowl and add the veal. Be sure that the veal is completely covered with the marinade. Cover the bowl and refrigerate overnight.
3.   When ready to serve, heat the butter in a skillet and brown the livers lightly. Add the veal, basil, thyme, garlic, salt and pepper to the pan. Brown the veal quickly on both sides. Cover the veal and livers with the prosciutto, then lay the mozzarella and esrom cheeses alternately over the prosciutto. Add the wine, cover the pan and cook until the cheeses melt. Sprinkle with the parsley and serve immediately.

Note: The perfect cut of the veal for this preparation comes from the top round of the leg. Once this piece has been freed from its membrane and connective tissue, it is cut across the grain into ⅛-inch-thick slices.

Medaglioni di Vitello con Porcini e Peperoni

Medallions of Veal with Porcini and Peppers

Serves 4

½ cup dried porcini mushrooms or any fresh wild mushrooms

1 large sweet red pepper

24 ounces veal medallions (from rib eye) cut ¾ inch-thick

4 tablespoons clarified butter (page 309)

½ cup Barolo wine

2 tablespoons Espagnole Sauce (page 271)

8 whole savory leaves
Salt and freshly ground black pepper

1.   Cover the porcini mushrooms with tepid water and let them soak for 1 hour. Drain and rinse the mushrooms, then cut them into thin slices. If using fresh mushrooms, simply clean and cut them into thin slices.

2.   Scorch the skin of the pepper over a flame of the burner (or broiler). Peel the skin and cut the pepper into ¼-inch-wide strips.

3.   Pound the medallions lightly.

4.   Heat the butter in a skillet. Add the medallions and brown them on both sides. Add the wine and Espagnole Sauce and reduce for 1 minute. Add the red pepper and simmer for 2 minutes. Add the mushrooms, savory and salt and pepper to taste.

5.   Remove the medallions to a warm serving plate. Continue to reduce the sauce until it is a syrupy consistency; then spoon it over the veal and serve immediately.

Scaloppine di Vitello alla Marsala
Veal Sautéed with Marsala
Serves 4

1⅓	cups cream sherry	½	lemon
⅔	cup water	4	tablespoons Marsala
2	garlic cloves, finely chopped	1	teaspoon finely chopped garlic
	Freshly ground black pepper	2	teaspoons dried basil
20	ounces veal wafers (see Note)	2	tablespoons finely chopped
½	cup clarified butter (page 309)		fresh parsley leaves
⅔	cup dry sherry	4	lemon wedges for garnish
1⅓	cups thinly sliced fresh mushrooms		

1.   Start the marinade the day before.

2.   Combine the first 4 ingredients in a bowl and add the veal wafers. Be sure the veal is covered completely with the marinade. Cover the bowl and refrigerate overnight.

3.   Heat a large skillet over high heat. Add 4 tablespoons of the dry sherry to the hot pan, tipping the pan so that the sherry coats the bottom evenly. Add the clarified butter and heat it. Add the veal and the mushrooms to the pan and sauté the veal very quickly on both sides. Remove the veal and mushrooms from the pan and keep them warm.

4.   Keeping the pan on high heat, squeeze the lemon juice into the pan, then add the remaining sherry, Marsala, garlic and basil and cook over high heat until it is reduced to a syrupy consistency. Return the veal to the pan and coat it quickly with the sauce.

5.   Arrange the veal on a warm serving dish and add the sauce and chopped parsley. Serve immediately with the lemon wedges.

Note: The perfect cut of the veal for this preparation comes from the top round of the leg. Once this piece has been freed from its membrane and connective tissue, it is cut across the grain into ⅛ -inch-thick slices.

Bistecca con Porcini
Beefsteak with Porcini and Brandy
Serves 4

2	ounces dried porcini mushrooms	4	tablespoons clarified butter (page 309)
4	cups tepid water	4	garlic cloves, finely chopped
4	16-ounce New York shell steaks, trimmed of excess fat (Leave ¼-inch of fat.) Salt and freshly ground black pepper	4	teaspoons finely chopped shallots
		½	cup brandy
		½	cup beef stock (page 63)
		2 to 4	tablespoons butter, softened

1.   Cover the porcini with the tepid water and let them soak for 1 hour. Remove the porcini and rinse them very well. Cut them into thin slices. Strain the soaking liquid through several layers of paper towels and reserve it.

2.   Preheat the broiler.

3.   Rub salt and pepper into both sides of each steak. Broil them, turning once, to the desired doneness.

4.   While the steaks are cooking, prepare the sauce. Heat the clarified butter in a saucepan. Add the garlic and shallots and sauté for 30 seconds. Add the brandy and allow it to burn off, about 1 minute. Add the porcini, stock and ¼ cup of the soaking liquid from the mushrooms. Allow to reduce over high heat for 2 minutes or until thickened.

5.   Transfer the steaks to a warm serving dish.

6.   Add the butter to the sauce and lower the heat to moderate. Quickly whisk the butter into the sauce, pour it over the steak and serve immediately.

NOTE: This sauce is also excellent with grilled veal chops. Simply substitute veal stock for the beef stock.

Bistecca alla Piemontese
Beefsteak Broiled with Mushrooms and Red Wine
Serves 4

4	16-ounce New York shell steaks, trimmed (Leave ½ inch of fat.)		Salt and freshly ground black pepper
6	tablespoons clarified butter (page 309)	1	cup thinly sliced fresh mushrooms
4.	garlic cloves, pressed	½	cup dry red wine
		2	teaspoons fresh lemon juice

1. Preheat the broiler.
2. Rub both sides of the steaks with the butter, garlic, salt and pepper. Place the steaks in a shallow pan. Broil until one side of the steak is well browned. Turn them over, add the remaining ingredients and broil to the desired doneness.
3. Transfer the steaks to a warm serving dish and top with the mushrooms and pan juices.

Filetti di Bue Capricciosi
Fillets of Beef with a Little of Everything
Serves 4

MARINADE

2	tablespoons extra virgin olive oil	8	whole black peppercorns
½	cup dry red wine	1	teaspoon dried basil
2	teaspoons dry mustard	1	teaspoon chopped fresh ginger
		4	4-ounce beef fillets

SAUCE

4	anchovy fillets, rinsed and dried	2	teaspoons dry mustard
4	tablespoons chopped green olives	1½	cups dry red wine
		4	slices pancetta
8	fresh basil leaves		Salt and freshly ground black pepper

1.   Mix together all the ingredients for the marinade in a bowl. Add the beef and marinate at room temperature for 2 to 4 hours.
2.   Blend the anchovy fillets, olives, basil, mustard and ¼ cup of the wine until smooth.
3.   Remove the beef from the marinade and rub it with salt and pepper.
4.   In a heavy skillet, render the fat from the pancetta. Remove the pieces of meat. Add the beef and brown for 2 minutes on each side. Spread the anchovy-olive paste on the top of the fillets. Continue to cook over moderate heat to the desired doneness.
5.   Remove the beef from the pan. Scrape any pieces of meat from the pan. Add the remaining red wine and let it reduce until syrupy. Season with salt and pepper and pour the sauce onto a warm plate. Arrange the beef fillets on top and serve immediately.

*C*iro and Sal's is open year 'round, though only on weekends in winter. Tourists swell Provincetown's population from 4,000 in winter to 20,000 during the height of summer. Still, the climate in winter is generally mild enough to allow walks on the beach in February. The pace slows to a gentle shuffle but the town does not collapse into winter hibernation.

Pòlpette
Meatballs
Makes 12 Meatballs

2	tablespoons olive oil		2	tablespoons dried basil
1½	cups bread crumbs		¼	cup finely chopped fresh
1	cup milk			parsley leaves
1	pound lean ground beef		⅓	cup freshly grated Parmigiano
2	large eggs			Salt and freshly ground black
½	cup dark raisins			pepper
½	teaspoon finely chopped garlic			

1.   Preheat the oven to 400 degrees.
2.   Coat the bottom of a baking pan with the olive oil.
3.   Mix the bread crumbs with the milk in a bowl and let them stand to absorb the milk.
4.   Add the remaining ingredients to the bowl and mix well.
5.   Use a tablespoon to scoop out the mixture. Form into 1-inch balls. Arrange the meatballs in the pan and add ¼ cup of water to prevent the meat from sticking to the pan.
6.   Bake for about 20 minutes.

NOTE: If desired, transfer the meatballs to another pan, add 1 recipe Ragù (page 117) and bake for 10 minutes more.

Agnello al Ferri con Carciofi Fritti
Broiled Lamb Chops with Fried Artichokes
Serves 4

1	cup dry sherry	4	¾-inch-thick lamb chops
	Juice of 1 lemon	1	cup bread crumbs
4	tablespoons extra virgin olive oil	½	cup freshly grated Parmigiano
		4	large eggs
2	garlic cloves, finely chopped	½	cup milk
1	teaspoon chopped fresh rosemary leaves	12 to 16	artichoke hearts, steamed until tender
	Salt and freshly ground black pepper	1	cup olive oil
		4	lemon wedges

1.   Combine the first 6 ingredients in a pan just large enough to fit the lamb chops. Marinate the chops at room temperature for 4 hours.

2.   While the lamb is marinating, prepare the artichokes.

3.   In a shallow pan mix together the bread crumbs, cheese, salt and pepper.

4.   In a bowl, beat together the eggs, milk, salt and pepper.

5.   Dip the artichokes in the egg wash, allowing the excess egg to drip off, then roll them in the bread crumbs.

6.   Heat the oil in a skillet and fry the artichokes until they are golden all over. Drain on paper towels and keep them warm.

7.   Place the lamb chops and the marinade in a shallow pan. Broil the lamb chops to the desired doneness, turning them once.

8.   Transfer the chops to a warm serving dish. Boil the marinade 2 minutes and pour over chops. Serve with the fried artichokes and lemon wedges.

Lombata di Maiale
Roast Loin of Pork with Zinfandel Sauce
Serves 8 to 10

1	4- or 5-pound pork loin, boned	2	cups coarsely chopped watercress (stems removed)
	Salt and freshly ground black pepper	3	garlic cloves, crushed
8	thin slices esrom	¾	cup olive oil or rendered pork fat
8	thin slices prosciutto	1	cup veal stock (page 64)
3	garlic cloves, finely chopped		

SAUCE

8	tablespoons butter	¼	teaspoon dried thyme
2	carrots, coarsely chopped	1	cup seedless red grapes, coarsely chopped
1	large onion, coarsely chopped		
¼	cup red Zinfandel wine		

1.   Preheat the oven to 325 degrees.

2.   Cut the loin in half lengthwise. Season both halves with salt and pepper. Sprinkle the chopped garlic on one of the halves, lay the slices of esrom over the garlic, lay the prosciutto over the cheese and spread the watercress over the prosciutto. Take the other half of the loin, seasoned side down, and lay it on top of the watercress. Tie the two halves securely together with string. Rub the outside of the tied loin with the crushed garlic and more salt and pepper.

3.   Heat the oil in a large skillet and brown the loin on all sides. Remove the loin from the skillet and place it in a roasting pan. Add the veal stock to the pan and place it in the preheated oven. Roast the pork for 20 minutes per pound, basting it occasionally.

4.   About 20 minutes before the meat has finished cooking, prepare the sauce. Melt the butter in a skillet. Add the carrots and onion and sauté until the vegetables are tender. Strain ¼ cup of the stock and drippings from the roasting pan and add it to the skillet with the vegetables. Add the Zinfandel and the thyme and let reduce for about 5 minutes.

5.   Strain this sauce into another pan and add the grapes. Cook over low heat for about 5 minutes. Adjust the seasoning if necessary and keep warm. Once the pork loin has finished cooking, remove it from the oven and let it sit for 5 minutes. Slice the pork and serve it with the sauce and additional sprigs of watercress.

Rognoni Trifolati
Veal Kidneys Sautéed with Prosciutto and Red Wine Vinegar
Serves 4

4	veal kidneys	½	cup red wine vinegar
4	tablespoons red wine vinegar	2	teaspoons chopped fresh basil leaves
4	tablespoons olive oil	½	teaspoon dried marjoram
1	cup thinly sliced onion		Salt and freshly ground black pepper
4	thin slices prosciutto, fat removed and cut into small pieces		

1.   Skin the kidneys and remove all tubes and fat. Cut the kidneys into ½-inch cubes. Immerse them in cold water to which you have added 4 tablespoons vinegar and some salt. Let soak for 1 hour, then drain and rinse the kidneys, and pat them dry.

2.   Heat the oil in a skillet or rondo and sauté the onion until it is brown and glazed. Add the prosciutto and kidneys. Lower the heat and cook for 2 minutes, stirring. Add the remaining ingredients and continue to simmer until the kidneys are cooked (not pink but still tender).

3.   Serve the kidneys with the sauce spooned over them.

Coniglio alla Modenese
Braised Rabbit with Porcini Sauce
Serves 4

MARINADE
½　cup extra virgin olive oil
1　onion, chopped
2　carrots, chopped
2　celery stalks, chopped
6　ounces prosciutto, sliced and
　　cut into ¼-inch pieces
½　cup red wine vinegar
3　cups dry white wine
6　fresh sage leaves

2　bay leaves
⅛　teaspoon chopped fresh
　　rosemary leaves
2　garlic cloves
½　teaspoon whole black
　　peppercorns
　　Salt
2　rabbits, dressed and quartered

½　cup olive oil
¼　pound butter
4　tablespoons tomato paste
2　cups dry sherry
2　ounces dried porcini
　　mushrooms

1　garlic clove, finely chopped
　　Salt and freshly ground black
　　pepper
　　Fresh parsley and arugula for
　　garnish

1.　Make the marinade the night before: Heat the oil in a saucepan. Add the vegetables and half of the prosciutto and sauté until tender. Add the vinegar, wine, herbs and spices and bring to a boil. Lower the heat and simmer for 10 minutes. Remove from the heat and let cool.

2.　Place the rabbit pieces in a pan and pour the marinade over them. Cover and marinate at room temperature for 8 to 10 hours.

3.　Remove the rabbit from the marinade and pat dry. Heat the oil and half of the butter in a large heavy skillet. Brown the pieces on all sides. Add the remaining prosciutto and cook slowly 10 minutes.

4.   Strain the marinade and add it to the skillet. Stir in the tomato paste and sherry. Cover the pan, lower the heat and cook slowly for 45 minutes.

5.   While the rabbit is cooking, soak the mushrooms in 2 cups of tepid water for 40 minutes. Drain and rinse the mushrooms well, and pat them dry.

6.   Heat the remaining butter in a skillet. Add the garlic and sauté for 30 seconds. Add the mushrooms, season with salt and pepper, and sauté for 2 minutes.

7.   Arrange the rabbit on a warm serving platter. Remove the pieces of prosciutto from the pan and sprinkle them over the rabbit. Then arrange the mushrooms over and around the rabbit. Pour the sauce from the pan over all. Garnish with sprigs of fresh parsley and arugula.

UOVA
Eggs

onservation is not a new concept to the folks of Provincetown. The "Province Lands" were set aside as a natural reserve way back in 1654. Today the National Park Service oversees the Cape Cod National Seashore, almost 44,000 acres of protected wild area. Once Henry David Thoreau walked these bogs and dunes. Now four million visitors a year marvel at the beauty of this spectacular sweep of coastline.

Frittata
Italian Omelet
Serves 1

2 to 3 tablespoons olive oil or clarified butter (page 309)

Salt and freshly ground black pepper

1 teaspoon finely chopped fresh parsley

1 small garlic clove, finely chopped

1 teaspoon finely chopped shallots

3 large eggs

Freshly grated Parmigiano

1. In a bowl beat the eggs, salt, pepper and parsley together.
2. Heat the oil in an omelet pan. Add the garlic and shallots and sauté for 30 seconds over high heat. Add the eggs. As the eggs set, lift the sides of the frittata so that the uncooked egg will flow under and cook. When almost all of the egg is cooked, either add the filling, or if it is to be a plain omelet, continue to the final step.
3. Place a plate over the pan and flip the frittata over onto the plate. Slide the frittata back into the pan and cook for 1 minute longer. Sprinkle with Parmigiano and serve immediately. The frittata is not folded in half as with the French omelet; instead, it is served as a flat circle.
4. An alternative to flipping the frittata is to place it 2 inches below a preheated broiler for 30 seconds.

NOTE: Any range of fillings can be added to the frittata; your imagination is the limit. Here are some suggestions: sautéed zucchini; sautéed zucchini with fresh tomatoes and basil; fresh tomatoes, mozzarella and basil; Pecorino; thinly sliced sautéed potatoes and rosemary; prosciutto and sautéed mushrooms; shrimp and chives; sausage; sausage, roasted peppers and onions; black olives, goat cheese and fresh tomatoes; pancetta and potatoes; ricotta, fontina and Parmigiano. The possibilities are endless. These fillings may be mixed in with the beaten eggs or layered on top while the frittata is still cooking on the first side.

The frittata may also be sliced into wedges and served with Ragù or Simple Tomato Sauce (page 115).

It can be served as a hot or cold antipasto. It is also excellent rolled inside a veal roast.

*C*iro's restaurant is the kind of place that people return to again and again when they want to celebrate very special occasions. One couple who had dined there on their honeymoon returned ten years later on the wife's birthday. The husband's surprise gift for her was a pair of beautiful gold hoop earrings which were in his pocket when they arrived for dinner.

Now, Ciro's wait staff have always been known to be arty, interesting characters — painters, actors, gays, each with their own unique flair. In fact, the couples' waiter that night sported three gold hoop earrings of his own.

As they waited for dessert to be served, the husband quietly drew one of the earrings from his pocket and slipped it under his wife's napkin. The waiter arrived, set their desserts on the table and bustled away. When the wife lifted her napkin she exclaimed in surprise, "Oh, look, our waiter dropped his earring!"

Frittata con Pasta
Pasta Omelet
Serves 4 to 8

This is an excellent way to use leftover sauced or unsauced pasta. Of course, it may also be made with freshly cooked pasta.

10	large eggs	1	pound pasta cooked al dente
½	cup freshly grated Parmigiano		(fettuccine, spaghetti, penne,
	Salt and freshly ground black		fusilli, etc. work well.)
	pepper	¼	cup olive oil
2	tablespoons chopped fresh	2	garlic cloves, chopped finely
	parsley leaves		Extra sauce (optional)

1.   Separate 4 of the eggs. Save the whites. Add the yolks to the remaining 6 eggs and beat well. Add the Parmigiano, salt and pepper, and parsley to the eggs and mix well.

2.   Pour the egg mixture over the pasta. Toss well.

3.   Beat the egg whites until stiff and fold them into the pasta.

4.   Heat the oil in a large cast-iron skillet. Add the garlic and sauté briefly over high heat. Pour the pasta mixture into the pan and smooth it into an even layer (it will probably be 2 inches thick). Cook over high heat for 10 minutes. Lower the heat and continue to cook for another 10 minutes.

5.   If possible, place a large plate over the pan and flip the frittata over onto the plate. Slide the frittata back into the pan. Raise the heat and cook until the egg is set (about 15 minutes). The outside should be crispy. The frittata may also be baked in a hot (400-degree) oven if flipping is unmanageable.

6.   Remove the frittata from the pan, slice it into wedges, and serve with extra sauce. If it was plain pasta (unsauced), use a sauce of your choice (the

tomato-based sauces work best). If using plain pasta, some sauce may also be added to the pasta before frying. You should vary the seasonings according to your tastes. Fresh herbs work wonderfully.

This may be served as an antipasto, first course or light main course.

Zucchini con Uova e Formaggio
Zucchini with Eggs and Cheese
Serves 4

4	tablespoons olive oil	¼	cup freshly grated Parmigiano
½	cup finely chopped onion		Salt and freshly ground black
4	small zucchini, cut into thin		pepper
	rounds	2	tablespoons chopped fresh
½	cup chicken stock (page 65)		chives
4	large eggs		

1.   Heat the oil in a skillet. Add the onion and sauté until it is golden and glazed. Add the zucchini, stir and cook for 5 minutes. Add the chicken stock and salt and pepper to taste. Cook until the zucchini is al dente.
2.   In a bowl, beat together the eggs, cheese, salt and pepper.
3.   Remove the pan with the zucchini from the heat. Pour the egg mixture into the pan and stir well to set the eggs. Serve garnished with the chives.

Uova Lessate
Hard-Boiled Eggs with Olive Oil
Serves 4

This may be served as an antipasto or light main course.

8   large eggs
4   tablespoons extra virgin olive
    oil

Salt and freshly ground black
pepper
8   anchovy fillets (optional)

1.   Hard-boil the eggs, being careful not to overcook; the yolks should
be yellow, not gray. (See Glossary.)
2.   Peel the eggs and slice them in half lengthwise. Sprinkle the oil over
them and season with salt and pepper. If desired, rinse the anchovy fillets,
dry them well and drape them over the eggs.
3.   Serve immediately with good crusty bread and perhaps a green salad
and cheese.

Uova al Piatto con Patate e Prosciutto
Eggs Baked with Potatoes, Mozzarella and Prosciutto
Serves 6

	Butter		Salt and freshly ground black
6	small red or white potatoes		pepper
6	thin slices prosciutto		About 2 tablespoons grated
½	pound mozzarella, thinly sliced		Parmigiano
6	large eggs	2	teaspoons of butter

1.   Preheat the oven to 400 degrees.

2.   Butter the inside of a baking dish large enough to hold 6 eggs without crowding them.

3.   Boil the potatoes until they are tender, then peel and cut them into thin slices.

4.   Layer the potatoes over the bottom of the baking dish. Layer the slices of prosciutto over the potatoes, and then layer the mozzarella over the prosciutto. Crack the eggs into the pan, keeping them evenly spaced. (You will have a whole egg on top of the layers of potato, prosciutto and cheese.) Season with salt and pepper and sprinkle with the grated cheese. Cut 2 teaspoons of butter into small pieces and distribute it over the eggs.

5.   Bake for a few minutes, or until the whites of the eggs have set. Serve immediately.

Uova al Piatto con Prosciutto e Gruviera

Eggs Baked with Prosciutto and Gruyere

Serves 6

	Butter	3	ounces Gruyere, grated
6	large eggs	2	tablespoons freshly grated
6	thin slices prosciutto, cut into		Parmigiano
	¼-inch-wide strips	4	teaspoons butter, melted
	Salt and freshly ground black		
	pepper		

1.   Preheat the oven to 400 degrees.

2.   Butter a baking dish. Break the eggs into it, keeping them separate. Arrange the strips of prosciutto around the yolks. Sprinkle with the Gruyere and then the Parmigiano and dribble the melted butter over all. Bake for a few minutes, or until the whites of the eggs have set. Serve immediately.

Uova al Piatto alla Toscana
Eggs Baked with Spinach and Balsamella
Serves 6

2	pounds fresh spinach, leaves only		Salt and freshly ground black pepper
4	tablespoons butter		Pinch of freshly grated nutmeg
½	medium-size onion, finely chopped	6	large eggs
8	tablespoons grated Parmigiano	1	cup Balsamella (page 267)

1.   Wash the spinach leaves and place them in a large saucepan. Cover the pan and cook the spinach, without additional water, over low heat until it has wilted. Drain the spinach and squeeze out any excess liquid. Chop the spinach finely.

2.   Preheat the oven to 350 degrees.

3.   Melt the butter in a skillet and add the onion. Sauté until it is translucent. Add the spinach. Stir and sauté for another minute. Remove from the heat and season with salt, pepper and nutmeg. Then mix in 8 tablespoons of the Parmigiano.

4.   Butter a round baking dish. Arrange the spinach in a ring along the outer edge of the dish. Break the eggs into the center of the bowl, keeping them separate. Cover the eggs with the Balsamella. Sprinkle with the remaining Parmigiano and bake for about 15 minutes, or until the whites of the eggs are set. Serve immediately.

NOTE: This can also be done in individual ceramic dishes. A variation would be to use a tomato sauce (page 115,116).

Uova Sode e Fritte
Hard-Boiled Eggs Stuffed with Ricotta and Fried
6 Servings

6	hard-boiled large eggs, peeled and cut in half lengthwise	1	large egg, beaten and seasoned with salt and pepper
¾	cup whole milk ricotta	½	cup (approximately) dry bread crumbs
1	heaping tablespoon grated Parmigiano	¼	teaspoon dried oregano
	Pinch of ground nutmeg	½	teaspoon dried basil
	Salt and freshly ground black pepper	1½	cups olive oil
½	cup (approximately) all-purpose flour, seasoned with salt and pepper		

1.   Remove the yolks from the eggs and mix them well with the ricotta, Parmigiano, nutmeg and salt and pepper to taste. Stuff the mixture back into the cavities where the yolks had been and over the white of the egg also. You should have a smooth mound over the cut surface of the egg. (It will be almost the size of a whole egg again.) Once you have done this with all the eggs, roll each very carefully in the flour. (Pat back into shape with a knife, if necessary.) Then dip each in the beaten egg and roll them very gently in the bread crumbs which have been seasoned with the oregano and basil, being careful to cover them completely.

2.   Heat the oil in a skillet with high sides. (Do not let the oil smoke.) Fry the eggs until they are a deep golden color. Drain on paper towels and serve immediately.

ORTAGGI E LEGUMI
Vegetables

*N*ew Orleans may be famous for Mardi Gras but Provincetown carries the spirit all through the year with gaudy parades, outlandish costumes and great parties. P' Town is never without a reason to celebrate beginning with its own Mardi Gras- complete with costume balls and festivities at clubs and inns all over town. July 4th is celebrated with parades and floats and spectacular fireworks on Town Wharf. In late July droves of costumed celebrity look-alikes light up Hollywood Night, a benefit for the Provincetown Rescue Squad. In August, the Provincetown Business Guild stages Carnival, a week of special events, with nightclub shows, parties and a flamboyant parade of floats through the center of town. Come October, there's Fantasia Fair, an annual 10-day event with a talent show and a fabulous costume ball held on Halloween eve. Laissez le bon temps rouler, ma chere!

Legume alla Griglia
Grilled Vegetables
Serves 8

1	yellow bell pepper, sliced lengthwise	1	red onion, cut in eigths
1	green bell pepper, sliced lengthwise	2	zucchini, cut in rounds
		8	large mushrooms, sliced thick
1	red bell pepper, sliced lengthwise	¼	cup olive oil
1	eggplant, cubed if large, sliced if small		Salt and white pepper

1.   Put vegetables in a large crock. Add oil, salt and pepper. You can add crushed garlic if you wish. Let stand for 1 or 2 hours.

2.   Grill over charcoal, turning frequently. Basil makes a nice garnish.

Involtini di Pepperoni
Roasted Red Peppers with Mortadella and Anchovies
Serves 4

2	large roasted red peppers	¼	teaspoon marjoram
4	slices mortadella	8	leaves fresh basil
8	anchovies	¼	cup white wine
2	tablespoon capers	4 or 5	drops white wine vinegar
3	tablespoon olive oil		pepper to taste
1	clove garlic	1	lemon, sliced

1.   In a sauté pan heat olive oil, garlic and anchovies.

2.   When anchovies dissolve, add peppers and other ingredients. Cook for 5 minutes over low heat.

3.   If mortadella slices are large, cut into quarters. Arrange on a heated serving platter. Garnish with lemon slices.

Cuori di Carciofi Romanelli
Artichoke Hearts Broiled with Prosciutto and Parmigiano
Serves 4 to 5

20	artichoke hearts		Freshly ground black pepper
½	lemon	4	thin slices of prosciutto,
3	tablespoons clarified butter		trimmed of excess fat
	(page 309)	1½	tablespoons bread crumbs,
2	garlic cloves, finely chopped		seasoned with salt and pepper
¼	cup dry white wine	1½	tablespoons freshly grated
	Juice of ½ lemon		Parmigiano

1.   Preheat the broiler.

2.   Bring 2 quarts of water to a boil. Add some salt and the juice of ½ lemon to it. Put the artichokes into the water and cook until tender but not soft (al dente). Drain the artichokes and plunge them into ice cold water. When they are cold, drain them well.

3.   Heat the butter in a skillet. Add the garlic and sauté until it is golden. Add the artichokes, wine, lemon juice and black pepper. Cook the artichokes for about 7 minutes, stirring occasionally.

4.   Transfer the artichokes to an oven-proof dish. Arrange the slices of prosciutto over the artichokes. Combine the bread crumbs and grated cheese and sprinkle the mixture over the prosciutto.

5.   Place the pan under the broiler and broil just until the bread crumb and cheese mixture is browned.

Fagioli al Fiasco
Beans in a Bottle
Serves 4

Traditionally these beans were cooked in a bottle, but they can be cooked in a heavy casserole with equally good results. The beans are excellent with good crusty bread and wine for a simple meal. They can also be spread on Bruschette (page 22) for a simple meal or as an antipasto.

1	pound dried cannellini beans, sorted and rinsed	4 to 5 fresh sage leaves, stems removed
½	cup extra virgin olive oil	Salt and freshly ground black pepper
3	garlic cloves, pressed	

1.   Soak the beans overnight in cold water to cover. Drain and put them into a heavy 2-quart casserole. Add the oil, garlic and sage. Pour in enough water to cover the beans by 1 inch.
2.   Cover the pan tightly and set it over very low heat. Let the beans cook for about 2 hours, by which time almost all of the water and oil will be absorbed.
3.   Transfer the beans to a warm bowl. Season with salt and pepper and toss carefully.

NOTE: Another variation is to add 2 to 4 tablespoons of red wine vinegar to the warm beans for more of a marinated salad.

Lenticchie alla Napoletana
Lentils, Naples Style

1	bag lentils, washed and picked over	2	cloves garlic, minced
½	cup olive oil	2	quarts chicken stock, defatted
1	medium red onion, chopped coarsely	2	cups white wine salt and pepper
3	carrots, finely chopped		

1.   Soak lentils in cold water for 30 minutes.

2.   In a large heavy pot, sauté onions, garlic and carrots in oil. Cook for 10 minutes over low heat.

3.   Drain lentils and add to pot. Stir until lentils are coated.

4.   Heat broth and wine together. Add a little at a time to lentils. Continue until all liquid is added. Cover and simmer. If all liquid is absorbed before lentils are done add more broth or hot water.

5.   When lentils are soft, remove from heat and let stand 10 minutes before serving. Can be used as a starter, a side course or a dinner course.

Fagiolini con Prosciutto
String Beans with Prosciutto
Serves 6

1½ pounds young tender string beans	Salt and freshly ground black pepper
4 tablespoons butter	
6 thin slices prosciutto, excess fat removed	

1.   Remove the stems from the beans. Blanch the beans in salted water. Drain them and cool them in ice water. Drain again and dry the beans well.

2.   Melt the butter in a heavy skillet. Add the beans and toss to coat them with the butter and sauté for 3 minutes.

3.   Cut the prosciutto into ¼-inch squares and add it to the beans. Season with salt and pepper. Stir and sauté the beans over moderate heat until they are tender.

Broccoli al Crudo
Broccoli Sautéed with Oil, Garlic and Lemon
Serves 4

1	bunch fresh broccoli
¼	cup olive oil
2	garlic cloves, finely chopped
	Juice of ½ lemon
2	tablespoons dry white wine

Salt and freshly ground black pepper

Lemon slices or wedges for garnish

1.   Cut off the tough ends of the broccoli stems. Peel the stems to remove the tough skin. Blanch the broccoli in a small amount of boiling salted water; then plunge into ice cold water and drain well. Cut the broccoli into small spears, keeping the spears of equal size.

2.   Heat the oil in a skillet. Add the garlic and sauté until it is golden, then add the broccoli and the remaining ingredients. Cover the pan and cook over low heat until the broccoli is tender but not soft (al dente). Transfer the broccoli to a warm serving dish and pour the pan juices over it. Garnish with lemon slices and serve immediately.

Broccoli con Aglio e Olio
Broccoli Sautéed with Garlic and Oil
Serves 4 to 6

1 bunch fresh broccoli
2 tablespoons extra virgin olive oil
3 garlic cloves, thinly sliced
2 tablespoons dry white wine
Salt and freshly ground black pepper

8 to 10 black olives, sliced thinly lengthwise (optional)
2 to 4 ounces soft Pecorino Romano or goat cheese (optional)
Lemon wedges for garnish

1.   Cut off the tough ends of the broccoli stems. Peel the stems to remove the tough skin. Divide the broccoli into small spears of equal size.
2.   Blanch the broccoli in boiling salted water. Then plunge the broccoli into ice cold water to chill it and drain well.
3.   Heat the olive oil in a skillet. Add the garlic and sauté it over low heat until it is golden. Discard the garlic. Add the broccoli to the skillet and toss to coat each spear with oil. Cook for 2 minutes over moderate heat. Add the wine, salt and pepper, raise the heat and let the wine reduce to about 2 tablespoons. Cover the pan and cook over low heat until the broccoli is tender.
4.   If desired, the black olives and cheese may be added at the last moment. Serve immediately garnished with lemon wedges.

Broccoletti con Aglio e Olio
Broccoli Rabe Sautéed with Garlic and Oil
Serves 4 to 6

Broccoletti is often sold in the American markets under the name "rappini" or "broccoli rabe" or "rape." It is a dark green leafy vegetable with a slightly bitter taste. This preparation brings out the sweetness of the greens.

1	pound broccoletti	3	garlic cloves, thinly sliced
¼	cup extra virgin olive oil		Salt

1.   Wash the broccoletti in cold water. Cut off the bottoms of the stems if they are bruised. Cut the broccoletti into 1-inch pieces, leaving some of the small leaves whole.

2.   Heat the oil in a heavy skillet. Add the garlic and sauté until it is lightly browned, then discard the garlic.

3.   Add the broccoletti to the pan and toss to coat it with the oil. Lower the heat, cover the pan and cook the broccoletti only until it has wilted. Add the salt and continue to cook, uncovered, until tender. Stir occasionally.

Note: If you love garlic, do not discard it after it has browned.

Cavolini di Bruxelles con Pignoli
Brussels Sprouts with Pine Nuts
Serves 6

2	pounds brussels sprouts, with small compact heads	4	tablespoons butter
½	cup pine nuts		Salt and freshly ground black pepper

1.   Remove the stems and outer leaves of the brussels sprouts. Cut an 'X' into the base of each sprout (this aids in the cooking).

2.   Steam the sprouts until they are tender. Plunge the sprouts into ice water, then drain and dry them thoroughly.

Toast the pine nuts in a skillet over low heat until they are golden brown.

3.   Melt the butter in a skillet, then add the brussels sprouts, pine nuts, and salt and pepper. Stir well and sauté for 3 minutes. Serve immediately.

Cavolfiore al Romano
Cauliflower with Tomatoes and Parsley
Serves 6

1   head cauliflower
⅓   cup extra virgin olive oil
2   garlic cloves, peeled
2   parsley sprigs

2   plum tomatoes, peeled,
        seeded and finely chopped
        Salt

1.   Remove the core and outer leaves from the cauliflower and separate it into 1- to 1½-inch flowerets.
2.   Heat the oil in a heavy saucepan. Add the whole garlic cloves and let them cook for 1 minute (be careful not to let them burn). Add the cauliflower and the remaining ingredients to the pan. Lower the heat and cook the cauliflower slowly until it is tender, stirring gently from time to time.
3.   Discard the garlic and parsley and serve immediately.

Cavolo all' Agro e Dolce
Sweet and Sour Cabbage
Serves 6

1	head red cabbage	¼	cup red wine vinegar
5	tablespoons olive oil	¼	cup water
1	garlic clove, crushed and peeled		Salt and freshly ground black pepper
2	tablespoons honey		

1.   Remove the outer leaves from the cabbage. Cut it into quarters and remove the core. Cut each quarter into ¼-inch thick slices.

2.   Heat the oil in a large skillet. Add the garlic and sauté until it is golden, then remove and discard. Add the cabbage to the pan, cover and cook over moderate heat until it is wilted.

3.   Mix the honey, vinegar and water together and add the mixture to the cabbage. Season with salt and pepper, cover and cook until the cabbage is tender.

Finocchi alla Parmigiana
Fennel Sautéed with Butter and Parmigiano
Serves 4 to 6

2	small heads fennel	2	ounces freshly grated
5	tablespoons butter		Parmigiano
2	tablespoons dry white wine		
	Salt and freshly ground black		
	pepper		

1.   Remove the tops from the fennel bulbs and save them to use in soups. Trim the base of the bulbs and remove any tough or bruised outside layers. Cut the fennel bulbs into 1-inch-thick slices. Do not use any of the feathery greens in the core.

2.   Melt the butter in a skillet. Add the fennel and sauté for 5 minutes. Add the wine, salt and pepper and cook the fennel until tender. Sprinkle on the Parmigiano and serve immediately.

Funghi con Vino
Mushrooms Sautéed with Garlic and White Wine
Serves 4

4	tablespoons clarified butter (page 309)	½	cup dry white wine
2	garlic cloves, finely chopped	4	teaspoons finely chopped fresh parsley leaves
3	cups fresh mushrooms, sliced or quartered		Salt and freshly ground black pepper

1.   Heat the butter in a skillet. Add the garlic and sauté until it is golden, then remove the garlic and discard it. Add the mushrooms, parsley, salt and pepper to the pan. Stir and sauté for 3 minutes.

2.   Add the wine and cook for another 3 minutes. Serve immediately.

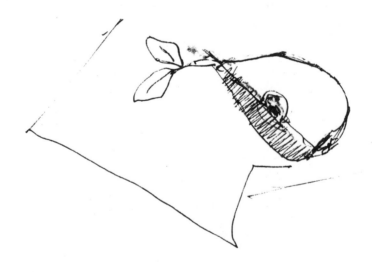

Funghi Affumicati
Smoked Mushrooms
Serves 4 to 6

This recipe was taught to me by my dear friend Genovina in Italy. The mushrooms are not actually smoked, but this is the name she gave me, so I shall use it here. They are delicious just the same.

1	pound wild mushrooms	2	tablespoons dry white wine
¼	cup extra virgin olive oil	1	parsley sprig
2	garlic cloves, peeled		Salt
1	plum tomato, peeled, seeded and finely chopped		

1.   Remove any tough stems from the mushrooms and wash them quickly in cold water. Do not dry them.
2.   Put the mushrooms in a heavy casserole pan with a little water over low heat. Cover and cook the mushrooms until they have expelled a good amount of liquid, 20 to 30 minutes. Discard the liquid.
3.   Heat the oil in another heavy casserole. Add the whole garlic gloves, lower the heat and sauté the garlic for 1 minute. Add the mushrooms and remaining ingredients and cook slowly until the mushrooms are quite tender, about 20 minutes. Stir the mushrooms carefully from time to time. Discard the garlic cloves and parsley and serve immediately.

Piselli con Prosciutto
Peas Sautéed with Prosciutto and Onion
Serves 4

1	cup chicken stock (page 65)
1	pound fresh peas (Thawed frozen peas can be substituted.)
3	tablespoons clarified butter (page 309)
¼	pound thinly sliced prosciutto, chopped
1	onion, finely chopped
	Salt and freshly ground black pepper

1.   Bring the chicken stock to a boil in a saucepan. Cook the peas in the stock until they are tender then drain the peas and save the stock for use in another dish.

2.   Heat the butter in a skillet. Add the prosciutto and the onion and sauté until the onion is translucent.

3.   Add the peas, salt and pepper and stir. Cook for 1 minute and serve immediately.

Patate Lessate
Boiled Potatoes with Olive Oil

Boil as many potatoes as you will need (usually 1 per person). When the potatoes are soft, remove them from the water and peel immediately. They may now either be mashed with a fork or riced (much prettier). Place on a warm serving plate and pour a generous amount of a good, extra virgin olive oil over the potatoes. Season with salt and pepper and serve immediately.

Bietole con Cipolle e Pomodori
Swiss Chard Sautéed with Onion and Tomatoes
Serves 6

2	pounds Swiss chard	2	tablespoons dry white wine
¼	cup extra virgin olive oil	6	plum tomatoes, peeled,
2	garlic cloves		seeded and finely chopped
1	onion, chopped or sliced thinly lengthwise		Salt and freshly ground black pepper

1.   Wash the Swiss chard in cold water and dry thoroughly. Trim the bottoms of the stems. Separate the stems from the leafy tops and cut the stems thinly on the diagonal. Roll the leaves and slice them thinly along the width.

2.   Heat the oil in a large skillet or saucepan. Add the whole garlic cloves and cook until they are golden, then remove and discard.

3.   Add the Swiss chard and the onion to the pan. Toss rapidly to coat the Swiss chard with the oil. Cover the pan and cook over low heat for 5 to 10 minutes, or until the chard has wilted. Add the remaining ingredients, stir and cook until the Swiss chard is tender.

NOTE: The onion and tomato may be omitted if a simpler dish is desired.

Pomodori Ripieni
Tomatoes Stuffed with Rice and Ricotta
Serves 6

6	large ripe tomatoes	2	tablespoons olive oil
1	cup Arborio rice	¼	cup ricotta or shredded fresh
¼	cup dry white wine		mozzarella
1¼	cups chicken stock (page 64)	2	ounces freshly grated
	Salt		Parmigiano
3	garlic cloves, finely chopped	6	fresh basil leaves, chopped
2	shallots, finely chopped		Freshly ground black pepper

1.   Preheat the oven to 400 degrees.

2.   Cut the tops off the tomatoes and set them aside. Carefully scoop out the seeds and pulp from the tomatoes. Pass the pulp through a sieve to remove the seeds and reserve.

3.   Put the rice, wine, stock and tomato pulp in a saucepan. Add salt to taste. Bring to a boil and cook the rice, covered, until it is very al dente (remember that it will be cooked again later). If there is any excess liquid, drain it from the rice.

4.   Remove the rice from the heat. Sauté the garlic and shallots in the olive oil for 2 minutes, then add them to the rice with the remaining ingredients and mix well.

5.   Season the inside of the tomatoes with salt and pepper.

6.   Fill each tomato with approximately ¼ cup of the rice mixture. Cover each tomato with its top.

7.   Arrange the tomatoes in an oiled baking pan. Pour a little olive oil over the tomatoes. Cover the pan with aluminum foil and bake for approximately 20 to 30 minutes. Serve immediately.

Zucchini con Basilico e Pomodori
Zucchini with Basil and Tomatoes
Serves 6

This is a summer dish that should be made only with fresh basil and the freshest, ripest tomatoes.

6   small zucchini
⅛   cup extra virgin olive oil
2   garlic cloves, thinly sliced
2   tablespoons dry white wine
2   large ripe tomatoes, cored
    and cut into ½-inch wedges

6   fresh basil leaves, stems
    removed
    Salt

1.   Wash and trim the ends off the zucchini, then slice it into thin rounds.
2.   Heat the oil in a skillet. Add the garlic and sauté until it is golden brown, then remove and discard.
3.   Add the zucchini to the pan and sauté for 5 minutes. Add the wine, tomatoes and salt. Stir gently and cook over moderate heat for 2 minutes. Add the basil leaves and cook until the zucchini is tender.

Zucchini Fritti
Fried Zucchini
Serves 6

2	medium-size zucchini	½	cup all-purpose flour
2	large eggs	2	cups bread crumbs
2	tablespoons milk	1	cup vegetable oil
	Salt and freshly ground black pepper	4	lemon wedges

1.   Wash and trim the ends off the zucchini, then cut it lengthwise into slices approximately ¼-inch thick. Discard the first and last slices.

2.   Beat the eggs and milk together in a shallow pan. Season with salt and pepper. Place the flour in another shallow pan and season it with salt and pepper also. Do the same with the bread crumbs.

3.   Submerge the zucchini slices in the beaten egg, then dredge them in the flour, shaking off any excess. Dip the slices once again in the beaten egg and then dredge them in the bread crumbs.

4.   Heat the oil in a skillet and sauté the zucchini slices on both sides until golden brown. Remove them from the pan and drain them on paper towels.

5.   Arrange the zucchini slices on a warm serving dish and garnish with the lemon wedges. Serve immediately.

NOTE: The better the bread crumbs, the better the crust. Make your own from good, crusty bread that has gone stale.

Ortaggi Arrosti con Aioli
Roasted Vegetables with Garlic Mayonnaise
Serves 4

1	small eggplant (The Japanese variety works well.)	1	garlic clove, finely chopped
1	small yellow summer squash	1	teaspoon fresh rosemary leaves, chopped
1	small zucchini		Salt and freshly ground black pepper
1	small head fennel		
⅓	pound wild mushrooms	½	cup Aioli (page 266)
½	cup extra virgin olive oil		

1.   Preheat the grill.

2.   Prepare the vegetables: Cut the ends off the eggplant, yellow squash and zucchini. Cut the vegetables into ½-inch wedges. Prepare the fennel as for the Finocchi alla Parmigiana (page 247), but do not cook it. Cut any tough stems off the mushrooms.

3.   Combine all the remaining ingredients except the Aioli in a large bowl or pan. Add the vegetables and toss well to thoroughly coat them with the oil. Allow them to marinate for 30 minutes to 1 hour.

4.   Grill the vegetables, turning them once, until they are tender, approximately 2 minutes on each side.

5.   Arrange the vegetables on a large platter and place the Aioli in the center as a dipping sauce or drizzle it over them.

NOTE: An alternate method is to braise the vegetables. Simply add ¼ cup of chicken stock and ¼ cup dry white wine to the marinade. Place the vegetables with the marinade in a roasting pan. Cover the pan and cook in a 400 degree oven until the vegetables are tender.

Remove the vegetables from the braised liguid and arrange them as you would for the roasted vegetables.

INSALATE
Salads

Insalata di Penne con Tonno e Broccoli
Pasta Salad with Tuna and Broccoli
Serves 4

1	bunch fresh broccoli	½	cup walnuts, toasted
1	pound white tuna or swordfish	4	garlic cloves, finely chopped
1	pound penne	2	tablespoons chopped fresh parsley leaves
4	ripe tomatoes, cored and cut into thin wedges		Salt and freshly ground black pepper
1	pound fresh mozzarella, cut into ¼-inch cubes	4	anchovy fillets, rinsed and dried
8	black olives, cut into thin slivers	¾	cup extra virgin olive oil

1.   Put a large pot of salted water on to boil for the penne.

2.   Separate all the broccoli flowerets from the stalks. Save the stalks for another use. The flowerets should be uniform in size (about 1 inch in diameter). Blanch the broccoli in the pasta water. When it is al dente, remove it from the water, transfer it to a bowl of ice water and drain thoroughly.

3.   If the tuna or swordfish is fresh, poach it in a little water with white wine and lemon juice. Let the fish cool and then break it into small chunks.

4.   Cook the penne in the salted boiling water until al dente. Rinse under cold running water until completely cooled, then drain well.

5.   Put the penne in a large serving bowl. Add all the remaining ingredients, except the anchovies and olive oil.

6.   Heat the olive oil in a small pan over low heat. Cut the anchovy fillets into small pieces, add them to the olive oil and mash them with a fork until they dissolve. Do not let the oil get too hot. Pour the oil and anchovy mixture over the salad. Toss very well and serve immediately.

Insalata di Pepperoni e Finocchio
Red Pepper and Fennel Salad
Serves 4 to 6

2	medium fennel bulbs	2	tablespoons good red wine
1	small red bell pepper		vinegar
8	large black olives		A few flakes of hot pepper
1	teaspoon minced parsley		Salt and freshly ground black
3	tablespoons virgin olive oil		pepper

1.   Trim the fennel, cut the stems to the top of bulbs. Slice crosswise, ⅛-inch thick. Soak in cold water ½ hour, drain and dry.

2.   Cut the pepper in half. Remove seeds and stem. Cut lengthwise into strips, approximately ¼-inch wide.

3.   Cut olives, discard pits, slice lengthwise. Place ingredients in a bowl and make a dressing with oil, vinegar, salt and red and black pepper. Toss and serve.

Insalata di Fusilli con Frutti di Mare
Pasta Salad with Seafood
Serves 4

½   pound shrimp, shelled and deveined

½   pound squid, cleaned and cut into rings

3   tablespoons dry white wine

¼   lemon

16   littleneck clams, washed

1   pound fusilli

¼   cup extra virgin olive oil

2   tablespoons finely chopped fresh parsley leaves

Salt and freshly ground black pepper

1 to 1½ cups cold Puttanesca Sauce (page 78)

1.   Poach the shrimp and squid in a little water with the white wine and lemon juice. Once they are tender, remove them from the pan and shock them in ice water and drain completely.

2.   Steam the clams until they open. Let them cool and remove them from their shells.

3.   Cook the fusilli in salted boiling water until it is al dente. Drain and cool completely under cold running water, then drain again.

4.   Put the fusilli in a large bowl. Cut the shrimp in half through the back; if they are large, cut the two sides in half again. Add the shrimp, squid and clams to the fusilli.

5.   Blend the Puttanesca Sauce, oil and parsley in a food processor until smooth.

6.   Add the sauce to the salad and toss well. Season with salt and pepper and serve immediately.

Insalata di Aragosta e Conchiglie
Lobster and Scallop Salad with
Basil-Ginger Mayonnaise
Serves 4

1	pound lobster meat, cooked	2	teaspoons grated fresh ginger
½	pound sea scallops	8	fresh basil leaves, chopped
2	tablespoons dry white wine	1	teaspoon fresh lemon juice
¼	lemon		Salt
1	cup Maionese (page 265)		Bibb or Boston lettuce leaves
1	garlic clove, finely chopped		

1.   Cut the lobster meat into ½-inch pieces. Poach the scallops in a little water with the white wine and lemon juice. Cool the scallops completely. If they are large, cut them in half.

2.   Blend all the remaining ingredients except the lettuce leaves in a food processor.

3.   Add the Maionese dressing to the lobster and scallops and toss very well. Serve on lettuce leaves.

NOTE: This also makes an excellent cold pasta salad. Simply add it to a pound of cooked fusilli.

Insalata di Lenticchie

Lentil Salad with Balsamic Vinegar and Mustard

Serves 6

1   tablespoon shallots, finely chopped

1   teaspoon garlic, finely chopped

1   tablespoon Dijon mustard

1½ tablespoons balsamic vinegar

2   teaspoons cream sherry

2   teaspoons dry vermouth

¼   cup extra virgin olive oil

Salt and freshly ground black pepper

1   recipe for Minestra di Lenticchie (page 53)

1.   Mix together the first 6 ingredients in a large bowl. Slowly whisk in the oil and season with salt and pepper.

2.   Drain the cooked lentils from the broth after step 2 (on page 53). Add them to the marinade while they are still hot and toss well. Reserve broth for another time. Let the lentils marinate for 30 minutes before serving.

Insalata Mista
Spinach and Arugula Salad
Serves 4 to 6

1	pound spinach, leaves only	Juice of ½ lemon
1	large handful arugula leaves	¼ cup extra virgin olive oil
1	Belgian endive	Salt and freshly ground black
8	fresh mushrooms	pepper

1. Wash the spinach and arugula and dry the leaves completely. Thinly slice the endive leaves on the diagonal. Thinly slice the mushrooms. Toss all the vegetables together in a large serving bowl.

2. Whisk together the lemon juice, olive oil, salt and pepper. Pour the dressing over the salad and toss well. Serve immediately.

Insalata di Radicchio e Cannellini
Radicchio and Cannellini Bean Salad
Serves 4

1 garlic clove, finely chopped
2 tablespoons red wine vinegar
¼ cup extra virgin olive oil
Salt and freshly ground black pepper

2 small heads radicchio
½ recipe for Fagioli al Fiasco (page 238—this must be started the night before)

1. Prepare the cannellini beans; you will have to start the night before.
2. Whisk together the garlic, vinegar, oil, salt and pepper. Let the dressing sit for 30 minutes.
3. Separate all the leaves of the radicchio and tear them into 2-inch pieces. (An alternative is to roll the leaves and slice them thickly across the width.)
4. Combine the beans and radicchio and toss well. Whisk the dressing, pour it over the salad and toss well. Serve immediately.

Insalata di Pomodoro, Basilico e Mozzarella
Tomato, Basil and Mozzarella Salad

1. Simply cut a pound of fresh mozzarella into ½-inch cubes and add them to the marinating tomatoes (recipe for Insalata di Pomodoro e Basilico) for the last 15 minutes.

Another option is to slice the mozzarella and tomatoes into rounds and arrange them in overlapping layers of mozzarella, tomato and basil leaf Pour the marinade over the center of the arrangement.

omatoes have also been called love apples and they grow in every back-
yard garden in Provincetown.

Some people maintain that the most romantic spot on the east coast is the
tip of the fish pier at sunset. Drowsy seagulls settle in for the night in the masts
of gently rocking fishing vessels. The dimming light at that hour drapes and
caresses all in its path. In summer the sunsets are radiant rose. In winter they are
searing red and orange. From the tip of the pier looking back at the town, the
sky and water merge in flames as lights slowly twinkle on in this quintessential-
ly quaint New England fishing village.

Insalata alla Napolitana
Neopolitan Salad of Tomatoes, Basil and Red Onion
Serves 4

4	large ripe tomatoes, cored and cut into ¾-inch wedges	2	garlic cloves, finely chopped
1	small red onion, cut into thin rounds	½	cup extra virgin olive oil
4	whole basil leaves	1½	teaspoons dried oregano
			Salt and freshly ground black pepper

1.   Combine all the ingredients and toss well but gently. Let marinate at
room temperature for 1 hour.

SALSE
Salad Dressings and Sauces

Interesting dressings can be made by adding various flavorings to a simple oil and vinegar mixture (2 parts oil to 1 part vinegar). Try adding mustard, fresh herbs, chopped scallions, shallots or garlic. Use flavored vinegars (tarragon vinegar for example). Whip Maionese or Aioli into any of the dressings below. Experiment, and if you are timid about putting two flavors together, try them in small amounts to see how they taste.

Salsa di Aceto e Olio
Salad Dressing
Makes 4 cups

1	cup red wine vinegar	2	teaspoons salt
1¼	tablespoons finely chopped garlic	1	teaspoon freshly ground black pepper
1½	tablespoons dried basil	3	cups olive oil
1½	teaspoons dried oregano		

1.   Whisk together all the ingredients or blend in a food processor or blender.

Maionese
Mayonnaise

6	large egg yolks	2	cups extra virgin olive oil, or
1	tablespoon fresh lemon juice		a lighter olive oil if you prefer
			a lighter Maionese
			Salt

1.   Put the yolks in a food processor and blend them. Keep the machine running and add the lemon juice, then add the oil very slowly. Once all the oil is added, season with salt. The Maionese will be very thick. If a thinner sauce is desired, a little water may be blended into the Maionese.

2.   If you add the oil too quickly and the Maionese breaks (becomes liquid), it can be saved. Remove the broken sauce from the processor. Place 2 more egg yolks in the processor and while blending, very slowly pour the broken sauce into the processor. This should get you what you're looking for.

Aioli
Garlic Mayonnaise

Add 2 to 4 cloves finely chopped garlic to the Maionese and blend.

MAIONESE

Use your imagination with Maionese and Aioli to make very interesting dressings. Here are some suggestions to get you going:

    Add fresh herbs (basil, rosemary, tarragon, parsley)

    Add saffron or curry

    Substitute vinegar for the lemon juice

    Use extra vinegar or a flavored vinegar

    Add extra lemon juice

    Add capers and anchovies

    Add roasted sweet red peppers

Balsamella
Besciamel Sauce
Makes 2 cups

4	tablespoons butter	1	bay leaf
4	tablespoons all-purpose flour		Pinch of nutmeg
1	cup milk		Salt and freshly ground
1	cup light cream		white pepper

1.   Melt the butter in a saucepan without letting it brown. Slowly whisk in the flour. Cook for 2 minutes over low heat, stirring constantly.

2.   Combine the milk and cream in another saucepan and heat it just to the boiling point. Do not let it come to a boil.

3.   Slowly add the milk to the butter-flour mixture, whisking constantly. Add the nutmeg, bay leaf, salt and pepper. Continue to cook the sauce over low heat, stirring constantly, for 5 minutes.

4.   If the sauce is not to be used immediately, lightly butter one side of a piece of wax paper and place it over the surface of the sauce (it should touch the sauce). This will prevent a skin from forming.

BALSAMELLA

This, like Maionese, can have many variations. Try adding:

Tomato paste
Sautéed onions
Sautéed mushrooms (sliced or chopped)
Fresh herbs
Blanched julienned vegetables
Puréed vegetables

Salsa Piccante
Piquant Sauce
Makes about ¾ cups

This is a Neapolitan sauce to which I have added a little Pommerey mustard. If you are a traditionalist, leave out the mustard. This sauce is excellent on fish cooked in any fashion or with boiled meats.

1	medium-size onion, finely chopped	1	thyme sprig, or ½ teaspoon dried thyme
⅔	cup Giardinera (page 13)	½	cup extra virgin olive oil
2	tablespoons capers, rinsed and drained	1	teaspoon Pommerey mustard
			Juice of ½ lemon
6	gherkins (not the sweet kind)		Salt and freshly ground black pepper
3	parsley sprigs (leaves only)		

1.   Finely chop together the first 6 ingredients. Put the mixture in a heavy-bottomed saucepan, cover and simmer over low heat for 1½ to 2 hours, or until all the ingredients are soft.

2.   Pass the mixture through a sieve and return it to the pan. Add the remaining ingredients and cook over very low heat for 10 minutes more.

*D*uring the time when Ciro was president of the Provincetown Art Association, fundraising was constantly on his mind. To help out, Norman Mailer, a frequent patron of the restaurant, agreed to read from his book, *Ancient Evenings*. The gala event, "a black velvet evening with Norman Mailer," drew a full house of 250 people including twenty-five who paid a premium to have dinner after the reading with Norman and his wife, Norris Church.

Norman, always generous in his support of the Provincetown community, was extravagantly munificent that evening. As midnight drew near, the reading continued apace and Ciro's cooks began to panic as the food got colder and colder.

Luckily, Norman looked out into the audience and noticed that the two youngest of his five children in attendance had fallen asleep.

Dinner with Norman ended at 3 a.m. with lively conversation to the last minute. The guests may have gotten heartburn from the elaborate repast they consumed at that late hour, but the Art Association benefited greatly.

Salsa Verde
Green Sauce
Makes ½ to ¾ cups

This sauce is delicious on fish. It can also be added to Maionese (page 265) and used as a dressing for cold fish dishes or seafood salads.

¼	cup fresh bread crumbs		Juice of ½ lemon
2	tablespoons red wine vinegar	½	cup fresh basil leaves (no stems)
¼	cup extra virgin olive oil	½	cup fresh parsley leaves
10	anchovy fillets		Freshly ground black pepper
2	hard-boiled egg yolks		

1.   Soak the bread crumbs in the vinegar for about 5 minutes. Squeeze any excess vinegar from the crumbs (use your hands to do this). Combine the bread crumbs with the remaining ingredients and blend in a food processor until smooth. Do not blend too long if you prefer a sauce with more texture.

NOTE: This sauce can be varied in several ways: 1) for a more piquant sauce, add 2 tablespoons of capers and one large clove of garlic, 2) add four leaves of fresh mint, 3) substitute tuna for the hard-boiled eggs or for half of the anchovies, 4) do all of the above.

Espagnole Sauce
Brown Sauce
Makes 1 Quart

We use this sauce often in our preparation of meats and in certain meat based stuffed pastas.

3	pounds veal bones	½	cup all-purpose flour
1	ham bone	3	cups dry white wine
1	large onion, stuck with 3 whole cloves	2	tablespoons tomato paste
½	cup clarified butter (page 309)	3	quarts water
3	garlic cloves, peeled and crushed	1	teaspoon whole black peppercorns, crushed
4	carrots, peeled and chopped coarsely	3	bay leaves
3	celery stalks, chopped coarsely	½	teaspoon dried thyme
		5	parsley sprigs

1.   Preheat the oven to 475 degrees.
2.   Put the bones and the onion in a roasting pan. Brown the bones in the oven for 30 minutes, turning them occasionally.
3.   Heat the butter in a saucepan and add the garlic, carrots and celery. Sauté over low heat for 10 minutes. Add the flour and stir for another 5 minutes. Stir in the wine and tomato paste. Raise the heat and bring the wine to a boil. Add all the remaining ingredients and bring the sauce to a boil once again.
4.   Add the sauce to the roasting pan with the bones and onion and return the pan to the oven. Lower the oven temperature to 275 degrees. Let the sauce cook for 5 hours, stirring occasionally.
5.   Remove the sauce from the oven and allow it to cool. Strain the sauce through a medium mesh strainer and discard the solids. The sauce can be frozen in small amounts for later use, or it can be tightly sealed and refrigerated for several days.

PANE E PIZZA
Bread and Pizza

Focaccia
Serves about 10

This is a flat bread that is actually like a pizza without the topping. The Italians eat it as a snack, either as is, or sliced in half with some thin slices of prosciutto between.

SPONGE

1	package active dry yeast	¾	cup tepid water
	Pinch of sugar	¾	cup unbleached white flour

DOUGH

1	tablespoon coarsely chopped fresh rosemary, or sage leaves (optional)	2	teaspoons salt
		3	tablespoons olive oil
		1	cup unbleached white flour

TOPPING

2	tablespoons extra virgin olive Coarse salt		Whole rosemary or sage leaves

1.   *Make the sponge:* In a large mixing bowl, dissolve the yeast and sugar in the water. Let the yeast sit until it begins to foam (this means that it is alive and working). Mix in the ¾ cup of flour and beat in an up and down circular motion (i.e., the down stroke goes through the center of the dough, and the up stroke comes up the side of the bowl). This stroke will help incorporate air into the dough. Using a wooden spoon, beat for 200 strokes. Cover the bowl tightly and set it in a warm (80 to 85 degree) place. Let the sponge rise until doubled, about 1 hour.

2.   Stir down the sponge and add the fresh herbs, salt and olive oil. (If you wish, omit the herbs and top the focaccia with coarse salt before baking.) Stir to blend. Add the flour and mix to get a smooth, soft dough. Turn the dough out onto a lightly floured board and knead it vigorously for about 8 minutes, or until it is smooth and elastic.

3.   Lightly oil the inside of a large mixing bowl. Form the dough into a ball and roll it around the inside of the bowl so that it is lightly coated with oil. Cover the bowl tightly and set it in a warm place. Let the dough rise until doubled, about 1 hour.

4.   Line the shelf of your oven with unglazed quarry (ceramic) tiles (available at tile stores) and preheat it to 500 degrees (it will take about 30 minutes). The tiles will hold the heat and are important to the baking process. Lightly flour a baking sheet.

5.   Punch the dough down and roll it out into an oblong or rectangular shape, ¼- to ⅛-inch thick. Lay the dough on the baking sheet. Sprinkle the remaining olive oil over the surface of the dough and spread it over the entire surface with your fingertips. Sprinkle with either the fresh herbs or the coarse salt.

6.   Bake for about 15 minutes, or until golden brown. The focaccia is best eaten immediatelv

Grissini
Very Thin Breadsticks
Makes 35 to 40 Breadsticks

⅔   cup tepid water
1   package active dry yeast
4   tablespoons olive oil
1   teaspoon salt

1½   cup unbleached white flour
¼   cup cornmeal
1   tablespoon crushed fennel seeds or chopped rosemary or sage leaves

1.   In a large mixing bowl, dissolve the yeast in the water and let sit until it begins to foam (5 to 10 minutes). Add the oil and salt to the yeast and stir to mix. Add 2 cups of the flour and beat with a wooden spoon for 100 strokes. Beat the dough using a vertical circular motion.

2.   Add the seeds or herbs, the remaining flour and the cornmeal. Mix thoroughly to get a soft dough that does not stick to the sides of the bowl. If the dough is sticky, add a little more flour.

3.   Turn the dough out onto a lightly floured board and knead vigorously for 5 to 8 minutes, or until the dough is smooth and elastic. Test its elasticity by pressing your thumb into the dough ball. If the indentation springs back, it is ready.

4.   Lightly oil the inside of a bowl large enough to accommodate the dough once it has doubled in size. Form the dough into a ball and roll it around the inside of the bowl so that it is lightly coated with oil. Cover the bowl tightly and set it in a warm place (80 to 85 degrees). Let the dough rise until doubled, about 1 hour.

5.   Grease a large baking sheet.

6.   Punch the dough down with your fist and turn it out onto a lightly floured board. Knead it for 30 seconds. Pull off half-dollar-size balls (the dough should yield about 35 or 40). Using the outstretched palms of your hands, roll out each piece until it is long and very thin (thinner than a pen-

cil). They will not all be perfectly shaped. Lay the sticks on the baking sheet, leaving ½ inch between them. Once all the sticks have been rolled out (or as many as you can fit on the baking sheet), let them rest for 30 minutes.

7.   While the dough is resting, preheat the oven to 325 degrees.

Place the baking sheet in the oven and bake the breadsticks until they are golden brown, 15 to 30 minutes.

Remove the breadsticks from the oven and let cool. Store them tightly wrapped in a cool, dry place or freeze in plastic wrap and aluminum foil.

Pane
Bread
Makes 2 Loaves

This recipe makes two round, crusty, yeast-flavored loaves. This bread must be started at least a day in advance.

STARTER

1.	package active dry yeast	½	cup whole wheat or rye flour
1	cup tepid water	½	cup unbleached white flour

SPONGE

2	cups tepid water	3	cups unbleached white flour

DOUGH

1	tablespoon salt	3½	to 4 cups unbleached white
2	tablespoons olive oil		flour.

1.   In a large mixing bowl (preferably a ceramic bread bowl), dissolve the yeast in the water. Let it sit until it becomes foamy. Add the flour and beat until smooth (use a wooden spoon). Cover the bowl tightly and set in a warm place (80 to 85 degrees) for 1 day. During this time, the mixture will bubble and expand and develop a strong yeasty odor.

2.   The next day, make the sponge. Add the water to the yeast mixture and stir to mix. Add the flour and beat for 200 strokes in an up and down circular motion. Cover the bowl and set it in a warm place.

If an especially yeasty flavor is desired, let the sponge sit for 1 day; otherwise, let the sponge rise until doubled in size, about 1 to 2 hours.

3.   Stir the sponge down and add the salt and olive oil. Stir to mix. Add the flour ½ cup at a time, mixing well after each addition, until you have a soft dough that no longer sticks to the sides of the bowl. Turn the dough out onto a floured board and knead vigorously for 10 to 12 minutes, or

until the dough is smooth and elastic (sprinkle the board and the dough with flour as necessary to keep the dough from sticking).

4. Lightly oil the inside of a large mixing bowl. Form the dough into a ball and roll it around the inside of the bowl so that the dough is coated lightly with oil. Cover the bowl tightly and set it in a warm place. Let the dough rise until doubled, about 1 hour.

5. Punch down the dough and divide it in half. Form each half into a ball. Lightly flour 2 kitchen towels on one side. Set each ball of dough on the floured side and wrap the towel around the dough. Let the dough rise for 30 minutes or until doubled.

6. While the dough is rising, line the oven shelf with unglazed quarry (ceramic) tiles and preheat it to 425 degrees (this will take 20 to 30 minutes). Lightly oil a baking sheet.

7. Transfer the loaves to the baking sheet, and using a razor blade or a very sharp knife, make 4 shallow slashes to form a square on the top of each loaf.

8. Bake the loaves for 40 to 50 minutes. To test for doneness, tap the bottom of each loaf. It will sound hollow when it is cooked.

9. Let the loaves cool completely on wire racks before slicing.

NOTE: These loaves also freeze well, wrapped in plastic wrap and aluminum foil.

Pizza

This recipe makes one thin-crust pizza about 12 to 14 inches in diameter.

DOUGH

1	package active dry yeast	3	tablespoons extra virgin olive
½	cup tepid water		oil
1½	cups unbleached white flour	1	teaspoon salt

TOPPING

10	anchovy fillets	12	ounces Italian plum tomatoes,
½ to ¾ cup (about 8 ounces)			peeled, seeded and chopped
	mozzarella, cut in small		Pinch oregano
	cubes or shredded		Salt and freshly ground black
			pepper

1.   In a small bowl, dissolve the yeast in the water. Let stand until it begins to foam.

2.   Sift the flour into a large mixing bowl and make a well in the center. Add the yeast mixture, 1 tablespoon of the olive oil and the salt to the well, and slowly incorporate them into the flour (use a wooden spoon). The dough should be soft and should not stick to the sides of the bowl (add more flour if necessary).

3.   Turn the dough out onto a lightly floured board and knead it vigorously for 6 to 8 minutes or until the dough is smooth and elastic. Lightly oil a mixing bowl (preferably ceramic). Form the dough into a ball and place it in the bowl. Roll the dough around so that it becomes lightly coated with oil. Cover the bowl tightly and set it in a warm place (80 to 85 degrees). Let the dough rise until it doubles, about 1 to 2 hours.

4.   Line the oven shelf with unglazed quarry (ceramic) tiles and preheat it to 500 degrees. Lightly oil a 14-inch pizza pan or a terra-cotta pan.

5.   Punch the dough down and turn it out onto a lightly floured board. Knead it for 30 seconds. Using your hands (this takes practice), flatten the dough and stretch it out into a circle (or rectangle, depending on your pan). Place the dough in the pan and push it with your fingers to fit the pan. Beat down the dough with your outstretched hand until it is ⅛- to ¼-inch thick and fits the pan. If the dough extends over the sides of the pan, tuck it under itself to form an edge.

6.   Sprinkle 1 to 1½ tablespoons of olive oil over the dough and smooth it over the entire surface. Arrange the anchovies, mozzarella and tomatoes over the surface (or use any of the toppings listed below). Leave a plain border about ½-inch wide. Sprinkle on the oregano, salt, pepper and remaining olive oil.

7.   Bake for 20 to 30 minutes or until the crust is golden and crispy.

OTHER TOPPINGS:
  Sautéed onions
  Raw whole egg (place it in the center of the pizza)
  Hard-boiled eggs, sliced thinly or chopped
  Sautéed peppers, mushrooms, etc.
  Sautéed eggplant
  Pre-soaked porcini mushrooms
  Pre-soaked sun-dried tomatoes
  Provolone, Pecorino, ricotta, Parmigiano, goat cheese
  Prosciutto, salami or sausage
  Chopped raw clams seasoned with fresh parsley and oregano
  Fresh basil and fresh tomatoes
  Tuna
  Capers

Pizza Fritta
Fried Dough

Serves 4 to 6

1 cup water	2 teaspoons active dry yeast
2 tablespoons olive oil	3 cups all-purpose flour
1 teaspoon salt	4 cups vegetable oil
1 teaspoon sugar	Granulated sugar or honey

1.   Combine the water, olive oil, salt and sugar in a small saucepan and heat until lukewarm. Remove from the heat and add the yeast. Stir to dissolve the yeast and let stand for 5 to 10 minutes (if the yeast is active, it should be foamy by this time).

2.   Sift the flour into a mixing bowl. Make a well in the flour and pour the yeast mixture into the well, slowly mixing the flour into the liquid. Once all or almost all of the flour has been used, turn the dough out onto a lightly floured board and knead for 3 to 4 minutes, or until it is smooth and elastic.

3.   Place the dough in a lightly oiled bowl, cover it tightly, and set it to rise in a warm place for 1 to 2 hours, or until doubled in bulk.

4.   Punch down the dough, turn it out onto a lightly floured surface and divide it into 10 or 20 pieces (depending on what size you desire). Form each piece into either balls or flattened circles.

5.   Let the pizze (doughs) rest while you heat the oil in a deep skillet. Use a piece of one of the dough balls to test the temperature of the oil—it should fall to the bottom and then rise quickly to the surface.

6.   Have paper towels ready for draining the pizze. Heat the oven to keep the pizze warm once they have been cooked.

7.   Fry the pizze a few at a time (they should have space around them in the pan). Fry them until golden on one side, then flip them over and cook until golden on the second side. Remove them from the oil with a slotted spoon and set them to drain on the paper towels. Then keep them warm

on a heat-resistant plate in the oven.

8.   Once all of the pizze have been fried, sprinkle them with granulated sugar or drizzle honey over them and serve immediately.

9.   If you want to have these for breakfast, the dough may be left to rise in the refrigerator overnight. The next morning you can divide the dough and let it come to room temperature. Fry the pizze and serve with the sugar or honey.

NOTE: These pizze can also be served as a light lunch or dinner. Follow the directions for preparing the pizze but instead of the sugar or honey, place on each pizza a spoonful of the sauce from the Penne all' Arrabiata recipe (page 97). Sprinkle with freshly grated Pecorino and place in a hot oven until the cheese melts. Serve immediately.

DOLCI
Desserts

*D*uring the first years of the restaurant, the desserts were mostly fresh fruit. Because Ciro and Sal did not have a liquor license, they put spirits in the desserts—peaches in red wine, pears in port, figs in brandy.

Ciro's wife Ero wanted to create a dessert that was luscious but still refreshing, as fruit is after a heavy Italian meal. After some experimentation, she created a pie that combined the creaminess of ice cream, the crunchiness of graham crackers and the tartness of lime. It was an instant success. Parfait Gelato has remained the most requested dessert on the menu for forty years. Steady customers still call in advance to make sure the lime pie is on the menu and will even go so far as to reserve a piece as extra insurance.

Parfait Gelato
Ice Cream Pie
Serves 16

½   gallon vanilla ice cream
1   cup lime-flavored gelatin powder
¾   cup fresh lemon juice
12 tablespoons sweet butter

3½ cups plain graham cracker
    crumbs
    Whipped cream
    Grated rind of 1 lime

1.   Let the ice cream sit at room temperature until it has softened (not melted) (about 30 minutes).

2.   Combine the gelatin powder and the lemon juice in a saucepan, bring to a boil and stir to dissolve the powder. Remove the mixture from the heat and let it cool.

3.   Melt the butter in a skillet and add the graham cracker crumbs. Stir well to thoroughly combine the graham cracker crumbs and the butter. Place half of this mixture in each of two 9-inch-round pie plates. Using a large spoon, press the crumb mixture into the pie form. The mixture should evenly cover the bottom and sides.

4.   Beat the gelatin-lemon juice mixture together with the ice cream until fluffy. Pour half of this into each pie form. Refrigerate the pies until they have set completely. Serve garnished with the whipped cream and grated lime rind.

Here are some additional flavors that can be substituted for lime:

LEMON: Follow the basic recipe, substituting lemon-flavored gelatine for the lime.

FRUIT: Follow the basic recipe, substituting lemon-flavored gelatin for the lime and using only ½ cup of lemon juice. Coarsely chop strawberries, peaches or pineapple and fold them into the pie mixture after the ice cream.

MOCHA RUM: Follow the basic recipe, substituting lemon-flavored gelatin for the lime. Use ½ cup of brewed coffee, to which a teaspoon of instant coffee has been added, instead of the lemon juice. Substitute chocolate ice

Cassata alla Siciliana
Pound Cake with Sweetened Ricotta and Chocolate
Serves 8

4	ounces semisweet chocolate	¼	cup mixed candied citrus peel
12	tablespoons sweet butter	¼	cup semisweet chocolate
½	cup brewed Espresso (Italian		shavings
	coffee)	1	pound cake (page 306)
1	pound ricotta	¼	cup Triple Sec
¼	cup confectioner's sugar		

1.   To make the frosting melt the 4 ounces of semisweet chocolate and the butter together in the top of a double boiler over simmering water. Stir to mix and then whisk in the Espresso. Remove the chocolate mixture from the heat and place it in the refrigerator. Stir every 15 minutes until it is smooth and firm.

2.   Mix together the ricotta, sugar and candied citrus peels. Beat until smooth, then fold in the chocolate shavings.

3.   Cut the pound cake twice lengthwise, creating 3 layers.

4.   Sprinkle half of the Triple Sec on the bottom layer. Spread half of the ricotta mixture on the pound cake (if you are using homemade, be sure that it is completely cooled). Top with the second layer and repeat the process. Top with the third and final layer.

5.   Cover the entire cake with ¼ inch of frosting. To do this, use a narrow cake spatula dipped occasionally in hot water.

6.   Serve at room temperature. This cake keeps well in the refrigerator.

Zuppa Inglese
Sponge Cake Layered with Rum and Zabaione
Serves 8 to 12

2	sponge cake layers (page 307)	12	large egg whites (Use the
1½	cups dark rum		yolks to make the Zabaione.)
½	recipe for Zabaione (page 289)	½	cup confectioner's sugar

1.   Preheat the oven to 400 degrees.

2.   Split each sponge cake layer in half to make 4 layers in all.

3.   Place the first layer on an oven proof serving dish and sprinkle it with one third of the rum. Spread one third of the Zabaione over the layer. Repeat with the second and third layers. Top with the fourth layer.

4.   Beat the egg whites, slowly adding the sugar, until they are stiff. Cover the cake entirely with the meringue, forming decorative peaks and swirls.

5.   Bake the cake for a minute or two, just until the meringue is browned.

Cannoli
Pastry Shells Filled with Sweetened Ricotta
Serves 6

1	pound (2 cups) whole milk ricotta	¼	cup semisweet chocolate shavings
¼	cup confectioners sugar	6	cannoli shells (may be purchased at Italian pastry shops or specialty stores)
¼	cup mixed candied fruit		
2	tablespoons creme de cacao		

1.   Beat the ricotta, sugar, candied fruit, and creme de cacao together until smooth and light. Fold in the chocolate.

2.   Fill the shells with the ricotta mixture. Arrange them on a serving dish and dust them with more confectioner's sugar. Serve immediately.

Crema Inglese
English Cream

This is my mother's recipe which I use for Zuppa Inglese.

2	cups heavy cream	¼	cup sugar
4	egg yolks	½	teaspoon pure vanilla extract

1.   Scald cream in a heavy saucepan.
2.   Whisk egg yolk and sugar until blended. In a slow stream add the hot cream to the egg mixture, whisking constantly. This is best when using a double boiler.
3.   Cook over medium heat until cream thickens or coats a spoon. Whisk constantly and do not allow to boil.
4.   Pour custard into a bowl set in ice. Stir until cool, then add the vanilla. Keep chilled until ready to use.

NOTE: For a different flavor, rum, brandy or liquors can be added.

Panna Cotta
Cooked Cream

Found in Northern Italy, from Sienna to Piedmont, this custard is delicious with fruit or berries.

1	package unflavored gelatin	½	cup confectioners sugar
4	tablespoons milk	¼	teaspoon pure vanilla extract
2½	cups heavy cream		

1.   Butter 6 small custard cups.
2.   In a bowl soften the gelatin in milk for 10 minutes.
3.   Combine the cream and sugar in a saucepan. Bring to boil. Stir over low heat to dissolve sugar, then add vanilla and gelatin. Stir briefly over low heat to insure gelatin has dissolved.
4.   Pour into custard cups and chill until set.

Zabaione
Marsala and Cream Custard
Serves 6

6	large egg yolks	1½	cups heavy cream
¼	cup sugar		Slivered almonds for garnish
1	cup Marsala		

1.   Put the egg yolks and sugar in the top of a double boiler. Beat with a whisk until they are light yellow. (Do not heat.)

2.   Bring water in the bottom of the double boiler to a boil, then lower the heat so that the water only simmers. Add the Marsala to the yolks and put the top of the double boiler over the simmering water. Stir constantly with a whisk or wooden spoon until the mixture coats the spoon. Be careful not to overcook. Remove from the heat and let cool completely.

3.   Whip the cream and fold it into the cooled mixture.

4.   Pour the zabaione into stemmed glasses and refrigerate for 1 hour. Serve with a sprinkle of slivered almonds.

Cuore di Panna
Heart of Cream
Serves 6

12	ounces cream cheese, at room temperature	1½	teaspoons vanilla extract
¾	cup confectioner's sugar	3	cups heavy cream
		1½	cups fresh strawberries, halved

1.   Beat the cream cheese, sugar and vanilla together until light and fluffy.

2.   Whip the heavy cream separately (it should be stiff), then fold the whipped cream into the cream cheese mixture.

3.   Line 6 heart-shaped porcelain molds (they must have perforated bottoms) with cheesecloth.

4.   Fill the molds with the cream mixture and smooth out the tops. Refrigerate for 3 to 4 hours.

5.   To serve, unmold the hearts onto cold serving plates and sprinkle with the fresh strawberries.

Zuccotto
Frozen Layers of Flavored Whipped Cream
Serves 1

1	pound cake (page 306)	1	teaspoon vanilla extract
¼	cup Triple Sec	1	teaspoon confectioners sugar
3	cups heavy or whipping cream	¼	cup mixed candied citrus peels
1	tablespoon brandy	⅓	cup finely chopped fresh
1½	ounces semisweet chocolate, melted and cooled		strawberries

1.   Cut the pound cake into ⅜-inch-thick slices. Cut each of these slices on the diagonal to get two triangles. Moisten each triangle with a sprinkle of the Triple Sec.

2.   Line a 2-quart round-bottomed bowl with the slices of cake. Start at the bottom of the bowl and work up the sides, covering the entire inside of the bowl.

3.   Whip 1 cup of the cream, the brandy and the chocolate until stiff. Pour the whipped cream into the cake-lined bowl and smooth it into a flat surface. Freeze the bowl until the cream has hardened.

4.   Whip the second cup of cream, the vanilla and the sugar until stiff. Fold in the candied citrus peels. Put this over the frozen layer of chocolate whipped cream. Smooth the surface and freeze until hardened.

5.   Whip the third cup of cream until stiff and fold in the strawberries. Pour it over the second frozen layer. Smooth the surface and freeze until hardened.

6.   When ready to serve, dip the bottom of the bowl in hot water for an instant. Place a cold flat dish over the top of the bowl and invert. The cake will fall out onto the dish. It should be a perfect dome.

7.   Cut the cake into wedges and serve on chilled plates.

Sufflè al Cioccolato
Chocolate Mousse
Serves 4 to 6

8	ounces semisweet chocolate	4	teaspoons dark rum or cognac
3	teaspoons brewed coffee	⅓	cup sugar
6	large eggs, separated		

1.   Put the chocolate and coffee in the top of a double boiler. Heat over simmering water until the chocolate has melted, then remove from the heat. Add the egg yolks and rum or cognac and blend until smooth. Let cool.

2.   Beat the egg whites until stiff, adding the sugar slowly. Fold the beaten whites into the chocolate mixture.

3.   Spoon the mousse into stemmed glasses and refrigerate for 1 hour.

4.   To serve, top with whipped cream and chocolate shavings, or whipped cream and grated orange rind, or both.

Pannettone di Cioccolata
Chocolate Amaretti Mold
Serves 12

FOR THE CARAMEL   ½   cup water
1½   cups sugar

1½   quarts milk   12   eggs, beaten
3   ounces semi-sweet chocolate,   1   cup sugar
      melted   ½   cup rum
4   tablespoons cocoa   Pinch of salt
7   ounces amaretti cookies,
      crumbled

1.   Preheat oven to 275 degrees.
2.   Place sugar and water in a pan. Cook over low heat, stirring constantly, until melted and turning a rich, golden color. Immediately pour into 6-ounce ramekins, turning to coat sides.
3.   In a large bowl thoroughly mix together all the remaining ingredients. Pour into ramekins. Fill to one inch from top. Place in shallow pan filled with boiling water and bake for 35 minutes or until set in center. Cool, then refrigerate. Serve cold.

Pannettone con Crema
Italian Bread Pudding
Serves 4 to 6

½	loaf of store-bought pannettone	4	whole cloves
3	cups heavy cream		Pinch of nutmeg
¾	cup sugar	11	egg yolks
1	vanilla bean	1	cup milk
1	cinnamon stick	2	oranges, peeled and segmented
		½	cup Port wine

1.   Preheat oven to 200 degrees. Remove crust from pannettone and discard. Cut into 1-inch cubes. Place on a baking sheet in oven for approximately 45 minutes to dry, not to toast.

2.   Heat heavy cream with sugar, vanilla bean, cinnamon, cloves and nutmeg. Bring to boil. Place egg yolks in a bowl and beat slightly until yolks are broken.

3.   Slowly pour heated cream over yolks, whisking constantly. Add milk. Pour mixture through a fine sieve into a clean container. Set in a bath of ice water to cool.

4.   Fill four 8-ounce ramekins with pannettone cubes. Pour custard into ramekins, until almost full. Let stand for 20 minutes to allow pannettone to absorb custard.

5.   Place ramekins in a roasting pan and add boiling water to pan, covering ⅔ of ramekin. Cover with foil. Cook one hour in preheated 300-degree oven. Remove foil and leave in oven, turned off, for 30 minutes. Remove from oven and cool at room temperature.

6.   Chill for 1 hour. Serve with orange segments soaked in Port wine.

Vanilla Pudding

Makes 3 cups

5	large egg yolks	2	cups milk or light cream
½	cup sugar	1	teaspoon vanilla extract

1.   In a mixing bowl, whisk together the eggs and sugar until they are light and foamy.

2.   Scald the milk or cream. Remove it from the heat and gradually whisk it into the egg and sugar mixture.

3.   Pour this mixture into a heavy-bottomed saucepan and place it over moderate heat. Heat just to the point before boiling, being careful not to let it boil. Lower the heat and continue to cook, stirring constantly with a wooden spoon, until the mixture coats the spoon. Remove from the heat.

4.   Stir in the vanilla and keep stirring until the mixture cools. If you do not want to use the pudding immediately, butter one side of a piece of wax paper and place it over the surface of the pudding. Refrigerate until needed.

NOTE: Various flavorings can be added to the pudding if desired: Substitute almond extract for the vanilla (use ¼ teaspoon); add grated orange or lemon rinds to the pudding while it is cooking; mix in toasted, chopped hazelnuts, walnuts or almonds.

Crostata alla Marmellata
Marmalade Tart
Serves 8

1¾ cups unbleached white flour	2 to 3 tablespoons heavy cream
½ cup sugar	12 ounces (about 1 cup) marmalade
8 tablespoons sweet butter, at room temperature	(peach, apricot and raspberry work well)
½ teaspoon grated lemon rind	1 teaspoon Triple Sec
1 large egg yolk	

1.   Lightly butter the bottom of a 9-inch tart pan with a removable bottom.

2.   Mix together the flour and sugar. Cut the butter into small pieces and add it to the flour. Quickly mix the butter into the flour. (The flour will have a sandlike texture when the butter is properly incorporated.)

3.   Mix the lemon rind into the flour, then make a well in the mixture and add the egg yolk. Slowly incorporate the egg into the flour mixture. Now do the same with the cream. Use only enough cream to hold the dough together.

4.   Form the dough into a ball, place it on a lightly floured surface and roll it out into a ¼-inch-thick circle. Fit the dough into the tart pan. The sides should be almost ½-inch-thick, and there should be no excess dough. Refrigerate the tart shell for 1 hour.

5.   In the meantime, preheat the oven to 400 degrees. Prepare the marmalade. Add the Triple Sec or liqueur of your choice to the marmalade. Heat it slowly and stir until smooth. Remove from the heat and set aside.

6.   Remove the tart shell from the refrigerator. Cover it with aluminum foil or parchment or wax paper, weight it down with dried beans or rice and bake the crust for 20 minutes. Remove the beans and foil and return the crust to the oven for another 20 minutes.

7.   Remove the tart shell from the oven and spread the marmalade over the center. If the edges are very brown, cover them with foil. Return the tart to the oven for 10 minutes.

8.   Remove the crostata from the oven and let it cool slightly before removing it from the tart form.

*A*rtist Leo Manso says he recalls "with nostalgia and pleasure Ciro's 'Family Table.'

The old pine table flanked by equally ancient benches on both sides (probably from the town dump), stood near the doors to the kitchen and was reserved for staff friends and artists—an underground artistocracy. It was not very comfortable, the ambiance was noisy and busy as hell, with artist-waiters continually going in and out of the kitchen, a constant ferment of activity.

Nevertheless, you always enjoyed sitting there—better than sitting on those little barrels with no backs, which hardened your rump while you devoured your pasta.

At any rate, while waiting for your order, you were constantly tantalized by the odors of Pasta Carbonara, Puttanesca, alle Vongole, etc., as the orders were carried from the kitchen to the patrons. By the time your order arrived, your taste buds had devoured all that passing food. The pasta was magnificent, and finally that great lime pie!

Not only that, Ciro generously poured you a brandy on the house!

Torta di Ciliege
Cherry Jam Tart
Serves 4 to 6

1⅓	cups flour	1	tablespoon powdered sugar
2	eggs	12	tablespoons butter, soft
¼	teaspoon salt	1	jar cherry jam
⅔	cup granulated sugar		

1.   Place flour on working area and form a bowl. Add one egg to the bowl with a pinch of salt. Add both sugars and soft butter, broken into bits. Quickly mix ingredients together by hand. Do not over knead. Roll into a ball, cover and refrigerate for 1 hour.

2.   Preheat oven to 425 degrees. Butter a tart pan. Place ⅔ of dough on floured counter, roll out in a circular shape the approximate size of the pan. Press into bottom and sides of pan. Spread with cherry jam.

3.   Roll out rest of dough and cut into ½-inch strips. Weave a basket pattern over top and brush crust with egg yolk. Bake for 40 minutes. Allow to cool before serving.

Crostata di Lampone
Raspberry Tart
Serves 6

This recipe is from Ruth, my sister-in-law. It is a pretty country tart, made with summer berries.

10	ounces pie dough, page 296	2	cups fresh raspberries
3	tablespoons sugar		Confectioners sugar

1.   Roll dough on a floured surface. Make an 11- to 12-inch circle. Place dough circle on a sheet pan, trim edges and sprinkle with sugar.

2.   Cover the dough with berries; leave a 2-inch border. Form circles with berries, extra ones pile in the center.

3.   Pull the dough border up and fold over the fruit. It should enclose the sides of the tart and pleat and drape over the fruit. Press down on dough. Be careful not to crush the fruit.

4.   Bake the tart in a preheated 450-degree oven for 20 to 25 minutes, or until the dough is a light golden color.

5.   Dust with confectioners sugar. Serve warm

Crostata di Mele
Apple Tart
Serves 8

1¾ cups unbleached white flour	2 to 3 tablespoons heavy cream
½ cup sugar	6 tablespoons apricot jam
8 tablespoons sweet butter, at room temperature	2 tablespoons water
½ teaspoon grated lemon rind	3 large Granny Smith apples
1 large egg yolk	2 tablespoons dark brown sugar
	1 tablespoon brandy

1.   Prepare the crust as for the Crostata alla Marmellata (page 295) up to the first baking.

2.   Preheat the oven to 400 degrees.

3.   Mix together the jam and water in a saucepan. Bring to a boil and cook for 3 minutes. Let cool.

4.   Peel and core the apples. Cut each in half and slice each half into ¼-inch-thick slices. Toss the slices in the sugar and sprinkle with the brandy.

5.   Brush the inside bottom of the tart with a thin layer of the jam. Arrange the apple slices in the tart shell. Brush with more of the jam if you want more of a glaze.

6.   Bake the crostata for 45 minutes.

7.   Fresh, very ripe peaches may be substituted for the apples. Bake the tart shell as for the Crostata alla Marmellata. After approximately 40 minutes of baking, remove the shell from the oven and brush the inside with a little marmalade. Arrange the peach slices in the shell and brush them with a little of the marmalade. Bake the tart 10 minutes longer.

Biscotti Semplici
Plain Biscuits
Makes 40 to 45 Biscotti

These are excellent with coffee or tea.

6	large eggs, separated	2	cups unbleached flour
1¼	cups sugar	1½	teaspoons baking powder
2	tablespoons liqueur of your choice (Amaretto or anisette are excellent.)	¼	cup walnuts or almonds, coarsely chopped

1.   Preheat the oven to 400 degrees.

2.   Lightly butter the bottom and sides of a 9-inch springform pan. Line the bottom with buttered parchment, or wax paper.

3.   Beat the egg yolks well and add the sugar. Continue beating until the mixture becomes light yellow, then add the liqueur and mix it in.

4.   In a separate bowl, beat the egg whites until they form soft peaks. Fold the egg whites into the egg yolk mixture. Add the flour and the baking powder a little at a time, and beat until the batter becomes smooth and light, about 2 minutes.

5.   Sprinkle half of the chopped nuts over the bottom of the springform pan. Pour in the batter and sprinkle the remaining nuts over the top.

6.   Bake for 20 to 25 minutes. The cake should be golden and slightly springy. Remove the cake from the oven and let it cool on a wire rack.

7.   Heat the oven to 450 degrees. When the cake is completely cooled, slice it horizontally to create 2 layers. Cut each layer into 2- by 1-inch rectangles.

8.   Place the rectangles on an unbuttered baking sheet, leaving a space between them. Bake the biscotti until they are a rich brown color. Turn them so all the sides brown evenly. When they are done cooking they will still feel a little springy but will harden as they cool.

Ricciarelli alla Crema Cioccolata
Almond Cookies with Chocolate Cream
Serves 6

8	ounces semi-sweet chocolate	3	tablespoons sugar
3	tablespoons milk	18	store-bought almond cookies
4	eggs		(amaretti)
½	tablespoon cherry brandy		

1.   Use a good chocolate. Melt the chocolate with the milk over a low flame or in a double boiler. Let cool.

2.   Beat egg yolks, brandy and sugar over low heat until very warm and slightly thickened. Cool, then combine with chocolate.

3.   Beat egg whites until they hold a peak. Gently fold into chocolate mixture. Pour the "crema" into 6 custard cups and freeze for 2 hours. Save the remaining cream.

4.   When ready to serve, heat cookies in a preheated 320 degree oven for 2 minutes. While hot, quickly dip cookies into chocolate cream. Do not saturate or cookies will beome limp.

5.   Remove frozen custard from cups. Place some of the remaining crema on plate, center the frozen chocolate cream. Surround with three cookies.

La Dolce Vita
The Sweet Life
Serves 6 to 8

1	pound cake (page 306) or an equal amount of ladyfingers	1	pound fresh strawberries
2	large very ripe peaches	2	cups vanilla pudding (page 232)
½	of a fresh pineapple		Ground cinnamon
2	large very ripe pears		Whipped cream

1.   Cut the pound cake into ½-inch-thick slices or split the ladyfingers. Line the bottom of a deep serving dish with the cake slices.

2.   Peel and seed the peaches and pears, and cut them into bite-size chunks. Cut the rind off of the pineapple and remove the core. Cut the flesh into bite size chunks. Hull the strawberries and slice them in half.

3.   Arrange one third of all the fruit over the first layer of cake. Cover the fruit with one third of the pudding. Sprinkle with cinnamon. Cover this with a layer of the cake slices and repeat the process until you have made a third layer and used all of the ingredients. Refrigerate for 1 hour.

4.   Serve in individual dessert glasses and top with softly whipped cream.

cream for the vanilla and add 3 tablespoons of rum to the ice cream.
COFFEE-BRANDY: Substitute lemon-flavored gelatin for the lime and ½
cup brewed coffee for the lemon juice. Substitute coffee ice cream for the
vanilla and add 3 tablespoons of brandy to the ice cream.

Ladyfingers
Makes 100

3	large eggs	1¼	cups unbleached white flour,
2	large egg yolks		sifted
¾	cup granulated sugar	¼	teaspoon grated lemon rind

1.   Preheat the oven to 400 degrees. Line a baking sheet with ungreased
wax paper.
2.   Bring a small amount of water to a boil in a medium-size sauce pan.
In a stainless steel mixing bowl, whisk together the eggs, egg yolks and
sugar. Place this bowl over the boiling water and lower the heat so that the
water barely simmers. Cook the mixture, stirring constantly with a wood-
en spoon, until it forms a soft foam and a spoonful of the batter poured
back into the bowl forms a "ribbon" (maintains some of its shape before
dissolving).
3.   Remove the bowl from the heat and stir the mixture until it is almost
cold. Fold in the sifted flour and grated lemon rind.
4.   Fill a pastry tube with the dough and squeeze finger lengths onto the
prepared sheet, leaving ½ inch between each finger. Bake for about 15
minutes.

NOTE: These freeze well when tightly wrapped in a plastic wrap.

Ciambella
Sweet Bread
Makes 1 loaf

This is a moist, cakelike bread that is excellent with rich Italian coffee.

1	cup milk	3¾	cups unbleached white flour
1	teaspoon honey	½	cup sugar
1	teaspoon active dry yeast		Pinch of salt
2	large eggs	2 to 3 teaspoons anise seeds	
4	teaspoons olive oil		

1.   Heat the milk until it is tepid. Stir the honey into the milk, then sprinkle the yeast into the milk and stir well to dissolve. Let stand for 5 to 10 minutes, or until the yeast is foamy (this means it is active).

2.   Beat the eggs and add them to the milk, then add the oil.

3.   Mix together the flour, sugar, salt and anise. Make a well in the flour and pour in the milk mixture. Using a wooden spoon, mix everything together and continue mixing in an up and down circular motion for 200 strokes.

4.   Cover the bowl tightly with plastic wrap and let it sit, away from drafts, overnight at room temperature (68 degrees).

5.   The next morning beat down the dough with a wooden spoon or your hand. Do this by turning the dough in on itself several times, adding a little more of the flour if it is very sticky.

6.   Turn the dough out on a lightly floured board. You will find that the dough is already quite elastic, so knead it lightly for only 2 minutes. Roll the dough into a thick log shape and form it into a ring. Join the edges well.

7.   Lightly butter a baking sheet and place the dough ring on it. Set the dough in a warm place and allow it to rise for 20 to 30 minutes.

8.   While the dough is rising, preheat the oven to 400 degrees.

9.   Bake the bread for 30 to 40 minutes. It will be golden colored and quite springy to the touch. Tap the bottom; it will have a hollow sound when it is done. Near the end of the baking period, brush the loaf with milk to give it a sheen.

10.   Let the bread cool completely on a wire rack before slicing.

Pound Cake

Makes 3 to 4 cakes

I can't remember where I found this recipe, but I have used it over the years to make a delicious, rich pound cake.

1	pound sweet butter	2	teaspoons vanilla extract
3	cups granulated sugar	1	tablespoon baking powder
6	large eggs cup milk or light cream	4	cups unbleached white flour

1.   Preheat the oven to 350 degrees. Butter and flour two 9- by 4- by 2-inch loaf pans.

2.   Cream together the butter and sugar until light and fluffy. Add the eggs one at a time and beat well after each addition.

3.   Sift together the flour and baking powder. In a separate bowl, mix together the milk and the vanilla. Add small amounts of the flour and milk mixtures to the butter mixture alternately, beginning and ending with the flour. Use a wooden spoon to blend after each addition. You do not need to beat this.

4.   Pour the batter into the prepared loaf pans. Bake for about 40 minutes. The top should be golden, and a toothpick inserted in the center should come out dry.

5.   Let the cakes cool in the pans for 10 minutes, then remove them from the pans and let them cool completely on wire racks.

NOTE: This cake freezes well when tightly wrapped in plastic wrap and aluminum foil.

Sponge Cake
Makes 2 cakes

10	large eggs	1	cup cornstarch
1¼	cups granulated sugar	7	tablespoons sweet butter,
½	teaspoon vanilla		melted
1	cup unbleached white flour		

1.   Preheat the oven to 425 degrees.
2.   Butter two 10-inch-round layer pans or a sheet cake pan. Line each with wax paper.
3.   Bring a small amount of water to a boil in a medium-size saucepan. Whisk together the eggs, sugar and vanilla in a stainless steel mixing bowl. Place the bowl over the boiling water and lower the heat so that the water simmers slowly. Cook, stirring constantly with a wooden spoon, until the batter forms a soft foam and draws into a ribbon.
4.   Remove the bowl from the heat and continue to stir until the batter is almost cool.
5.   Sift together the flour and cornstarch and fold it into the batter, then fold in the melted butter.
6.   Pour the batter into the pans and bake for 25 to 30 minutes. Turn off the oven and prop open the oven door. Leave the cakes in the oven for 5 minutes more.
7.   Remove from the oven. Turn the cakes out of the pans, let cool on wire racks and cool completely before slicing.

Gelato alla Crema
Ice Cream
Serves 6

5	large egg yolks	2	cups milk
⅔	cup sugar	2	teaspoons vanilla extract

1.   Beat the egg yolks with a whisk in the top of a double boiler or a mixing bowl large enough to fit over a pan of boiling water. Add the sugar and beat until the mixture becomes a very light yellow.

2.   In a separate saucepan, bring the milk just to the boiling point, but do not let it boil.

3.   Place the bowl with the egg-sugar mixture over a saucepan of boiling water. Lower the heat so that the water simmers slowly.

4.   Add the warm milk little by little to the eggs, whisking the milk completely into the eggs after each addition. Add the vanilla and continue cooking the mixture, stirring continuously with a wooden spoon until the mixture thickens slightly. When it is done, it should be the consistency of thin pudding and should coat the spoon. Be very careful not to overcook it, as the eggs will harden.

5.   Remove the bowl from the heat and set it in the refrigerator to cool. Stir occasionally to facilitate the cooling. Once it is cool, transfer the mixture to a loaf pan.

6.   Place the pan in the freezer and stir the gelato every 30 minutes for 2 hours. The finished gelato will be thick, smooth and soft. It should be served in smaller quantities than American ice cream, because it is quite dense.

GLOSSARY OF INGREDIENTS AND COOKING TECHNIQUES

Anchovies (Acciughe)

Buy anchovy fillets that are packed in olive oil, preferably an imported brand. Store any unused anchovies in their own oil, tightly wrapped in the refrigerator.

If you can find them, the whole, salt-packed anchovies are excellent. Wash off all the salt and bone the anchovies. To do so, slice down the belly and lift out the bone. You will be left with two fillets. Store any unused fillets in olive oil in the refrigerator. They will become too strongly flavored after 2 or 3 days, so use them immediately.

Bread Crumbs (Pangrattato)

To grate fresh bread crumbs, remove the crusts from slices of fresh Italian bread and rub the bread into the palm of your hand. This will crumble the bread sufficiently.

For dried bread crumbs, use stale bread and grate it in a food processor or blender until it is fairly fine. If you do not have any stale bread on hand, you can simply dry out slices of bread in a warm oven.

Butter (Burro)

In the recipes, I call for "butter" and "clarified butter." By butter I mean butter that has not been clarified. For baking, I always use sweet butter, but for cooking, lightly salted butter may be used.

I often specify to use clarified butter because it has a much higher burning point than whole butter (i.e., it can withstand higher temperatures); however, whole butter may be used instead of clarified if you are careful not to let it burn.

To clarify butter, melt at least 2 pounds of sweet butter in a heavy-bottomed saucepan. Once it has melted, you will be left with three layers: The top is a layer of white, foamy milk solids; the middle is the clarified butter; the bottom is water. Skim off the milk solids with a ladle and discard them. Ladle out the butter, being careful not to mix it with the water, and reserve it in a small saucepan. Throw away the water. This clarified butter may be stored tightly covered in the refrigerator and reheated as needed.

Cheese (Formaggio)

Cheese should be bought in small quantities that can be consumed within a few days. Always serve cheese at room temperature. Store any extra cheese tightly wrapped in plastic wrap and aluminum foil in the refrigerator; if the cheese will be eaten within two days, it can be tightly wrapped and left out of the refrigerator in a cool place. It is best to buy grating cheeses in small chunks and to grate them by hand as needed. Keep the chunks tightly wrapped in a cool, dry place. If a large quantity is needed, grate only the necessary amount.

Asiago: A delicately flavored cheese from Vicenza that is made from either whole or skimmed cow's milk. It has small holes throughout and is excellent as a table or a cooking cheese. The aged asiago is used for grating.

Bel Paese: A soft, mild cheese made from cow's milk. It is excellent both as a table cheese and as a cooking cheese.

Caciocavallo: A cow's milk cheese from Southern Italy. It is shaped like a sack and has a stringy (layered) texture. The semi-hard table cheese is delicate and sweet, while the hard grating cheese is sharp and robust.

Caciotta di pecora: A semi-hard, sweet cheese that is made from sheep's milk. It comes from both Sardegna and Central Italy and is good both as a table and a cooking cheese.

Caciotta: A soft cheese from central Italy. It is made from cow's milk and has a sweeter flavor than the caciotta made from sheep's milk.

Emmental: A cow's milk cheese from Switzerland. It is a semi-hard cheese with large holes and is sweet and flavorful. It is used both as a table and a cooking cheese.

Fior di Latte Treccia: A stringy, soft cheese much like mozzarella but made from cow's milk. It is slightly less flavorful than the mozzarella and is sold in braids. Store as you would mozzarella.

Fontina: A cow's milk cheese from Val d'Aosta. It is a semi-hard cheese with a sweet, delicate flavor. It is excellent both as a table cheese and as a cooking cheese.

Gorgonzola: A cow's milk cheese from Lombardy and Piedmont that is characterized by blue mold spores (much like blue cheese or roquefort). The soft Gorgonzola is mild and is excellent both as a table cheese and as a cooking cheese. The harder cheese is much more piquant and is excellent for the table.

Gruyere: Another Swiss cheese made from cow's milk but with a stronger flavor than emmental. It is a harder cheese that is often used in cooking, but it also makes an excellent table cheese.

Mascarpone: A very soft, buttery cheese with a sweet, delicate flavor. It is used in cooking and in desserts, as well as being an excellent table cheese.

Mozzarella di bufala: A stringy, soft cheese from Southern Italy. It is made from water buffalo's milk and has a sweet, slightly acidic flavor. It is excellent both as a table cheese and as a cooking cheese. It should be stored wrapped in paper in a bowl of water in the refrigerator. It will keep only a couple of days. It is available in small and large balls.

The mozzarella typically found in U.S. supermarkets is made from cow's milk. It is a harder cheese that is used in cooking or as the standard topping for pizza.

Mozzarella affumicata: Same as mozzarella but smoked.

Parmigiano-Reggiano: This is a hard cheese made from partially skimmed cow's milk. The yellower type is more delicate and is better as a table cheese, while the whiter version is better for grating. The grated Parmigiano-Reggiano can be used either alone or mixed with grated Pecorino Romano for a slightly more robust flavor.

Pecorino Romano: A hard cheese made from sheep's milk. It has a sharp, salty flavor and is excellent as a grating cheese (mix with grated Parmigiano-Reggiano if a milder taste is desired) or as a table cheese.

Pecorino Siciliano: A sheep's milk cheese from Sicily. It is flavored with black peppercorns and is a very hard, piquant cheese.

Provolone: A cheese made from cow's milk. When young (2 to 3 months) it is quite delicate and mild. Once aged, it becomes a much harder, sharper cheese. It has a stringy (layered) texture.

Ricotta Piemontese: A soft, very mild cheese that is made with the whey from cow's milk. It is excellent as a table cheese and for cooking or baking. It does not keep long, so keep it refrigerated and use it within two or three days.

In several recipes I say to squeeze the excess liquid from the ricotta. This is done by placing the cheese in some cheesecloth, gathering the cloth up around the ricotta, and twisting it tightly.

Ricotta Romana: The same as the ricotta piemontese but made with the whey from sheep's milk.

Romano: A cow's milk cheese made in the United States. It is a hard, strongly flavored cheese that is used for grating.

Scamorza: A semi-hard cheese from Southern Italy that is made from either cow's milk or a mixture of cow's and sheep's milk. It comes tied like a little bundle and is excellent as either a table or cooking cheese.

Scamorza affumicata: The same as scamorza but smoked.

Stracchino: A very soft, mild cheese from Lombardy. It is made from cow's milk and is used as both a table and cooking cheese.

Taleggio: A soft, cow's milk cheese from Lombardy. It has a slightly acidic flavor and is good both as a cooking cheese and as a table cheese.

Toma: A cheese from Val d'Aosta, Piedmont or Savoy that is made from whole or partially skimmed cow's milk. The younger cheese is strongly flavored, while the more aged cheese is sharp and salty.

Chicken (Pollo)
Buy fresh, not frozen, chicken because it is more succulent and tender. Cook within two days of purchasing it. Before preparing the chicken, rinse it thoroughly with cold water. Keep a separate cutting board for chicken and wash it and any utensils used to cut the chicken—as well as your hands—immediately after use. This minimizes the danger of infection by salmonella bacteria.

Whole chickens come in various weights, and some are more suited to certain preparations than others. Here is a guide:

Broiling chickens (broilers) weigh 1½ to 2½ pounds.

Frying chickens weigh 3 to 3½ pounds.

Boiling chickens weigh 4 to 5 pounds and are meatier.

Roasting chickens also weigh 4 to 5 pounds, are meaty and have quite a bit of fat

Cream (Panna)
Cream is called for in many of the recipes. Heavy cream will produce the richest, most flavorful result. For a lighter preparation use light cream, and if you must be diet conscious, use half-and-half; the reduction time on these sauces may be longer in order to thicken the sauce.

Eggs (Uova)
Always use the freshest eggs available and do not keep them long after purchase. Store eggs tightly covered in the refrigerator (the shells are porous and allow the passage of air into the egg). When cooking and baking, it is best to use eggs at room temperature, so remove them from the refrigerator at least 30 minutes ahead of time. Buy large grade 'A' brown or white eggs.

To boil eggs properly, place the eggs in a saucepan and cover them with cold water and a dash of vinegar. Bring the water to a boil and cook for 15 minutes. Remove the eggs from the water and place them in ice water for 5 minutes. Peel immediately or store unpeeled in the refrigerator.

Fat and Lard (Strutto e Lardo)

Rendered lard or pork fat is excellent for roasting and sautéing. Prosciutto fat can also be rendered for an even more flavorful fat, as can chicken fat, pancetta and bacon.

To render, place the lard or fat in a roasting pan in a slow (300 degree) oven. Allow the fat to melt slowly, and pour it off as it does. When the process is completed, only crispy pieces of meat or skin will be left. Store the rendered fat in a tightly sealed jar in the refrigerator.

In one recipe, I specify to blanch pork fat. To do this, bring a large pot of cold water to a boil, add ample salt and then add the strip of fat to the water. Do not let the water return to a boil. Let the fat blanch for 3 minutes. Remove it from the water, plunge it into ice water until it is completely cooled and pat dry with paper towels.

Fish (Pesce)

Always buy the freshest fish and shellfish available, preferably those varieties that are indigenous to your area. When buying fish, it should smell fresh, not fishy, the skin should be shiny and the flesh firm to the touch. If buying a whole fish, the eyes should be clear, the scales intact, the flesh firm and the gills red with blood. Have your fish merchant clean the fish for you. If a whole fish is required, leave on the head and tail. If you need fillets, ask for the head, tail and bones and use these to make your fish stock.

Cook fish only until it is opaque and the flesh flakes. The cooking time for a whole fish is about 10 minutes per inch of thickness (measure it at its thickest point). This time, however, is not an absolute, so test the fish as it cooks. Fillets will take an amazingly brief time to cook.

When purchasing clams, mussels and oysters, the shells should be tightly closed, and they should smell fresh. Wash them under cold running water, using a stiff bristled brush to scrub them. Mussels also have a "beard" that must be removed. The beard consists of several strands of fiber that protrude from the seam of the shell and serve to attach the mussel to rocks, etc. Remove the beard by giving it a strong pull, or pulling it up and out.

Cook mussels, clams and oysters only until the shells open. If they are particularly large, they may be cooked an additional minute or two.

If you purchase scallops in the shells, treat them as you would clams, etc. Usually, however, one purchases them already shelled. In this case, the scallops should be white or pink, fresh-smelling and firm to the touch. Clean the scallops by rinsing them in cold water and pulling off the small piece of muscle on the side (it will protrude slightly and be of a different texture). Cook scallops only until they are opaque.

You will most likely buy frozen shrimp (size 16 - 20) which must be thawed either in the refrigerator or under cold running water. If called for in the recipe, clean the shrimp by peeling off the shells, leaving the tails on. Save the shells to use in your fish stock or fish sauce. If desired, slice down the back of the shrimp and remove the intestine. Cook shrimp only until opaque.

These days one usually buys squid already cleaned. It should be porcelain-white or pink, firm and fresh-smelling. If you do buy whole squid, either fresh or frozen, you will have to clean it before cooking. To do this, pull to remove the head. Pull out the ink sac and cartilage and peel the dark outer skin from the body. Rinse it inside and out with cold water. You will be left with a clean, white sack that can be stuffed whole or sliced into rings or chunks. Pull the eyes and beak from the tentacles, wash the tentacles, and use them in your preparation. Cook squid until it is opaque and tender.

Purchase lobsters that are quite lively. The smaller (younger) ones will be more tender than the larger (older) ones. To boil a lobster, bring a large pot of cold water to a boil. Add the whole lobster head first to the pot and bring the water back to a boil. From that point, boil the lobster for 6 minutes per pound.

Flour (Farina)

I always use unbleached white flour for baking. All-purpose flour may be used in all other preparations. Flour can be measured by weight, using a small kitchen scale (which is more accurate) or in dry-measure measuring cups.

Fruit (Frutta)

Use only fruit that is in season and ripe. Fruit should be fragrant when ripe and have firm, sweet flesh. These days with insecticides, it is best to peel fruit before eating it. When using fruit in a cooked dish, it's better if the fruit is on the firm side rather than overripe

Herbs (Odori) and Spices (Aromi)

When possible use fresh herbs because nothing surpasses their taste. Fresh herbs are now available in many supermarkets and produce markets, but they are very easy to grow, either outside or inside. The herbs most commonly used in Italian cooking are rosemary, oregano, basil, sage and tarragon. If using dried herbs, check their potency by smelling them. They should be aromatic. Be careful in using dried herbs because they will usually be stronger and sharper in flavor than fresh herbs. Keep dried herbs tightly covered and stored in a cool, dry place. Preserve fresh herbs by wrapping them in damp towels and keeping them in the refrigerator. To keep fresh parsley (I prefer the Italian flat-leafed variety) and basil, keep them in the refrigerator with their stems in water. If possible, cover the leaves with a damp towel.

Spices also should be smelled to make sure that they are fragrant. Store spices tightly covered in a cool dry place.

Anise (Anice): A small oblong seed used in baking and in soup preparations. It is used crushed or whole and has a pleasant licorice flavor. Also called fennel seed.

Basil (Basilico): Fresh basil has broad, bright green leaves. It has a delicate, fragrant flavor and is wonderful in a wide array of summer dishes.

Dried basil is very strong with a slightly bitter taste, so use it sparingly.

Bay leaves or laurel (Lauro): This is a dried leaf that is dark green in color and highly aromatic. It is an essential ingredient in stocks, sauces, soups, marinades and meat roasts.

Capers (Capperi): The buds of the caper bush. They come preserved in brine or salt and must be rinsed very well before using. I prefer to rinse a quantity of capers and store them in dry white wine in the refrigerator. The wine gives them a milder, sweeter flavor. Capers add a special piquant accent to many dishes. I prefer the larger capers.

Garlic (Aglio): Only use fresh garlic. The bulb (head) of garlic should be plump, tightly packed and firm. When sliced, the cloves (individual pieces) should be highly fragrant. The more finely one slices or chops garlic the more flavor it imparts. In several recipes, I refer to pressing garlic. This imparts the strongest flavor and is done by using either a garlic press or a mortar and pestle.

Juniper berries: A fragrant, dried, blue-black berry that is used in marinades and in meat preparations. Available in specialty food shops.

Nutmeg (Noce moscata): A roasted nut about ½ inch in diameter. The more readily available form is ground, but if you can, go to a specialty food store and purchase the whole nut. Use a fine hand-grater or special nutmeg grater to grate the nut when needed. This will give the most flavor. Nutmeg is excellent in baking, as well as in sauces and meat and chicken dishes.

Oregano (Origano): Fresh Italian oregano has a small, round, green leaf and a delicate flavor. Dried oregano has a strong, sharp flavor, so use it judiciously. Dried oregano is excellent sprinkled over slices of fresh tomatoes and mozzarella that have been dressed with extra virgin olive oil.

Pepper (Pepe): If you do not have a pepper mill, buy one because the taste of freshly ground pepper far surpasses that of pre-ground. Freshly grind both black and white peppercorns. White pepper is less pungent but hotter than the black and will not add color to a white sauce. Peppercorns are available in supermarkets and specialty food shops.

Red Pepper (Peperoncino): When possible, buy the whole, dried red peppers and cut off small pieces as needed, otherwise crushed pods may be used.

Rosemary (Rosmarino): A long, thin, highly fragrant leaf. The fresh leaf is dark green and more subtly flavored than the darker dried leaf. If you use the dried rosemary in making a sauce, blanch it first. Rosemary goes well with meat, chicken, fish and vegetables.

Saffron (Zafferano): This is the dried stamen of the crocus flower. The strands are long and thin and the color should be red with only a little yellow. It is a very expensive spice, so use it judiciously. Be careful not to use too much saffron as it will give a medicinal taste; a small amount goes a long way and gives a mild, bittersweet flavor and yellow color to foods. Saffron is also used in bread baking.

Sage (Salvia): Only use fresh sage because the ground, dried herb gives a musty flavor. The leaves are grayish green, long and slightly fuzzy. Sage is wonderful in soups, sauces, marinades and roasts.

Tarragon (Dragoncello): A long, thin, olive green leaf that has a wonderful delicate flavor. The dried leaf is darker and slightly bitter, so use it judiciously.

Thyme (Timo): Fresh thyme is much more delicately flavored than the dried herb. If using the dried herb, use the leaf—not the powder. Thyme is excellent in stocks, soups and roasts.

Turmeric (Curcuma): This is purchased in ground form. Turmeric has a very mild, sweet flavor and imparts a strong yellow color to foods.

Meat (Carne)

Buy only the freshest meats and game, and have them cut and dressed as necessary by your butcher. Have him give you the bones and scraps to use in making stock.

Cured meats and sausages play an important role in Italian cooking, so acquaint yourself with the many varieties and special flavors.

Pancetta: This is a cured pork much like bacon. It has a higher meat content than bacon, however, and it is cured in salt and pepper. It also has a more delicate flavor, and for this reason, I prefer it for cooking. Bacon can, however, be substituted for pancetta. Purchase pancetta in Italian grocery stores or specialty food shops.

Prosciutto: Imported prosciutto is, of course, preferable to domestic, but our domestic variety is a fine substitute. When buying prosciutto, make sure that it does not have much fat and is a pinkish red color, not dark red. Have the prosciutto sliced paper-thin and ask the grocer for extra prosciutto fat (the scraps from the sliced meat); take this home and render it. If you can get the bone, too, use it for making soups.

Besides being used in cooking, prosciutto is excellent eaten with fruits like melon and figs or alone on a slice of crusty, coarse-textured Italian bread with olive oil sprinkled on top. Eat it as a sandwich with slices of salty focaccia (pizza bread) as the Italians do.

Sausages (Salsiccie): There are a variety of Italian sausages, but the most common are the sweet and hot sausages of southern Italy. I have used sweet sausages in the recipes in this book. In some of the recipes, I say to remove the sausage from its casing; do so by splitting the casing with a knife and removing the contents.

Salami: This is a name for cured meats such as mortadella and coppa: The meats are used in appetizers, cooked dishes, salads, sandwiches or as meals in themselves. Find a good Italian grocer for a variety.

Bresaola: This is a salt-and air-dried cured beef. Slice it thinly as with prosciutto and eat it sprinkled with extra virgin olive oil for an appetizer or light meal.

Nuts (Noci)

I use nuts extensively in cooking, so I like to keep a supply of almonds, walnuts and pine nuts on hand. Pistachios and hazelnuts come in handy, too. Store nuts in a cool, dry place in tightly sealed small amounts. They may also be frozen with excellent results.

Pine nuts are small, oblong, delicately flavored nuts from Italy. There is a Chinese variety that is shorter and plumper but with the same delicate flavor. Walnuts may be substituted for a similar flavor. Pine nuts can be purchased in any Italian grocery or specialty food shop.

Nuts are often toasted to bring out their flavor. To do so, place the nuts in a heavy-bottomed skillet and toast them over low heat or in a slow oven. Toss them continuously to keep them from burning. Once lightly browned, remove the nuts from the pan and let cool.

Olives (Olive)
When I specify black olives in cooking, I am referring to the Italian Gaeta olives or the Greek Kalamata. They should be firm, fleshy and sweet.

Two other types that I use often are the bitter Sicilian olives and the large, salty green olives. The Sicilian olives are small, black and wrinkled and are preserved in olive oil and red pepper. They have a strong flavor and are excellent with antipasti, cured meats, cheeses and bread.

The large, plump, green olives are excellent in antipasti and salads or in cooked preparations. Buy them with the pit in (not the pimiento-stuffed variety) and remove the pit if you are using them in cooking.

Olive Oil (Olio d'Oliva)
Good olive oil is essential to Italian cooking. The lighter imported virgin olive oils are readily available in supermarkets. This is an excellent all-purpose olive oil and is the one to be used in the recipes in this book, unless extra virgin olive oil is specified .

The extra virgin olive oils are fruitier (greener), more full-flavored and heavier than the virgin olive oils. The flavor and color of the oil will vary according to where it is made because not all olives are alike. Find an Italian grocer or a specialty food shop that carries a nice variety and experiment. These extra virgin olive oils are used in preparations in which the flavor of the oil is intrinsic to the overall flavor of the dish: salads, antipasti, Pasta alla Primavera, Spaghetti Aglio e Olio, Bruschette, etc. During the summer when ripe, fresh tomatoes are available, try sprinkling some extra virgin olive oil on a thick slice of coarse Italian bread and topping it with a thick slice of tomato and a sprinkle of salt. Delicious!

Pasta
Buy a good imported dried pasta instead of the domestic dried pasta. Several brands are now imported (DeCecco, San Martino, Agnesi, Martelli, etc.) and are available in many large supermarkets. If you have access to good quality fresh pasta, I would suggest using it occasionally with the lighter sauces or in "brodo" (broth or consommé). However, to my taste, the dried pasta usually has a better flavor and texture than the fresh.

Pasta comes in a seemingly endless variety of shapes and sizes. Try various shapes but remember that certain shapes are better for certain preparations. The tubular and shell shapes, for example, are most often used when the pasta is meant to hold or contain the sauce, as in cheesy pasta dishes, baked pastas, etc. Use the more interesting shapes (fusilli, ruote, etc.) to make beautiful and fun pasta salads.

Agnolotti: Half-moons of stuffed pasta. They are traditionally stuffed with meat or a sweet butternut squash mixture, but this can change according to one's imagination.

Bucatini: A long, thin macaroni that is hollow inside. It is excellent with fish-based sauces.

Capelli d' Angelo (Angel's hair): The thinnest spaghettini. A very fine, delicate pasta.

Ditali: Very short tubes of pasta (more like pieces of a tube).

Ditalini: Even smaller ditali. These are used in soups and broths.

Farfalle (Butterflies): A butterfly-shaped pasta that has little ridges along the edges.

Fettuccine: A broad, flat noodle typically used in cream sauces.

Lasagne: The broadest flat noodle with either a curly or a smooth edge. It is used in baked dishes.

Linguine: A long, thin pasta much like spaghetti but thicker and flattened (but not flat). I often use this instead of vermicelli or spaghetti.

Lumachelle: Short, curved lengths of grooved tubular pasta that looks like someone cut off from the tube and left the curve.

Mostaccioli: Similar to penne but with grooves. Also called penne rigate.

Penne: One-inch-long or shorter tubular pasta that is cut on the diagonal.

Ravioli: Stuffed squares of pasta. The filling depends on one's imagination.

Rigatoni: Large, grooved tubular pasta, two to three inches in length. The wider tubes are called "Occhi di lupo" or wolf's eyes.

Ruote: Wheel-shaped pasta (with spokes). These are fun to use in pasta salads.

Semi di mellone and Semi di cicoria: Tiny, seedlike pasta that is used in broths.

Spaghetti: The long, thin pasta with which most Americans are familiar.

Spaghettini: A thinner form of spaghetti.

Tagliatelle: Same as fettuccine but not as wide.

Tortellini and Tortelloni: Small, doughnut-shaped pastas. The tortellini are usually stuffed with a meat and cheese mixture, while the tortelloni, which are fatter, are usually stuffed with a spinach and ricotta cheese mixture or a sweet butternut squash mixture.

Vermicelli: A long, thin pasta like spaghetti but thicker.

Ziti: Long, smooth tubes of pasta. They come in various lengths and widths.

To cook pasta, bring an abundant amount of water (the pasta should not be crowded) to a boil and add a generous amount of salt (kosher salt dissolves better). Add the pasta to the water and stir to keep it from sticking together. (When cooking lasagne noodles, add a little olive oil to the water to keep the noodles from sticking together, which they do quite readily.) Cover the pot and return the water to a boil. Continue to cook the pasta at a boil, stirring often, until it is al dente (i.e., softened but still with a slight firmness or bite. Test for the right degree of doneness by biting into a piece of pasta.) This will take anywhere from about 6 minutes for the thinner pasta to 8 or 9 minutes for the thicker varieties. Fresh pasta will take 2 to 3 minutes, and stuffed, fresh pasta about 5 minutes.

Once the pasta is cooked, drain it immediately in a colander and transfer it to a warm serving bowl or platter. Add the sauce, toss and serve immediately. For certain preparations, you will cook the pasta briefly with its sauce before serving.

A word on serving sizes. Two ounces is the standard portion of pasta to be served as a first course. Double this portion if the pasta is served as a main course. The amounts will, however, depend on one's appetite: There are many people who can eat 4 ounces as a first course.

Polenta (Cornmeal)
Polenta is a staple of Northern Italy and is eaten, much as are rice and pasta, as a first course. It is also used as an accompaniment to strongly flavored dishes.

It is best to use imported Italian polenta, which can be found in Italian grocery stores or specialty food shops. American stone-ground yellow cornmeal may also be used with fairly good results. Store polenta tightly covered in a cool, dry place.

Rice (Riso)
When making Italian rice dishes, use imported Arborio rice, a short, white rice that comes from Northern Italy. If you cannot find Arborio rice in any Italian grocery or specialty food store, other brands may be substituted; the result, however, will not be the same. I have found that short-grained brown rice is the best substitute for taste and texture.

Tomato Paste (Conserva di Pomodoro)
Tomato paste is used to accent and heighten the flavor of tomatoes in sauces (it also thickens the sauce). When possible, buy the imported tubes of tomato paste, which allow you to use only what you need and then store the remainder easily. If you use the canned paste, freeze the extra paste in tablespoon amounts and use as needed.

Truffles (Tartufi)

This is a fungus that grows near the roots of shrub oak or beech trees. The truffle can be about the size and shape of a golf ball or larger and is either black (from France) or white (from Italy). Keep truffles stored in raw rice in a tightly sealed container in a cool, dry place.

Truffles have a slightly unpleasant odor when raw, but once cooked they lend a very special flavor to foods.

Vegetables (Ortaggi e Legumi)

Use only fresh vegetables and those that are in season. (Frozen peas are the only frozen vegetable that I find acceptable.) Vegetables should be firm or crisp. Avoid vegetables that have begun to shrivel or have brown spots on them. Leafy vegetables should have leaves that are richly colored, not yellow or brown, and are crisp, not wilted. The smaller, younger vegetables will be sweeter than the larger, more mature ones.

To keep leafy vegetables crisp, store them in damp towels or in a damp pillowcase in the refrigerator. Store root vegetables in a cool, dry place. Use vegetables shortly after purchase.

I often say to "blanch" a vegetable. I do this to preserve its color and to cook it only until tender or al dente. Bring a large pot of water to a boil. Salt the water and add the cut vegetable (always do white vegetables first) or put the vegetable in a wire basket and put this into the water. Bring the water almost to a boil, but do not let it boil. Cook (blanch) the vegetable just until tender (it should have a firmness to it). Drain and "shock" in ice water until the vegetable is completely cooled, then drain and pat dry.

Dried Beans (Fagioli Secchi): These are a wonderful food and an excellent source of protein. There is quite a variety of dried beans, so experiment with the various colors, shapes and flavors. Use them in both hot and cold dishes.

Many Italian recipes call for cannellini beans, which are white beans that look much like red kidney beans. Ceci or chickpeas or garbanzo beans are a nut colored bean with a delicate, nutty flavor. Lentils are a flat, dark green or brown, dried legume.

Beans can be purchased dried or already cooked and canned. I prefer to buy the dried beans because they are superior in taste and texture to the canned beans (the latter are also cooked with a good deal of salt). Simply sort (to remove any foreign objects) and rinse the beans, and then soak them overnight in an abundant amount of cold water. The next day, drain, cover with cold water and bring to a boil. Add a little salt to the water and cook the beans at a slow boil until tender (from 1 hour for cannellini beans to 2 or 3 hours for ceci beans).

Mushrooms (Funghi): A variety of mushrooms are now available in the better markets. If you can find them, try fresh chanterelles and morels; they can be used alone or mixed with domestic champignon mushrooms. Several of the recipes in this book call for the Italian porcini mushrooms. These come in dried form, are long and flat and are light brown in color. They give a distinctive, almost smoky or woody flavor to certain dishes. Soak the mushrooms in tepid water for 1 to 1 ½ hours before using. The porcini are also excellent mixed with fresh mushrooms and will give an added strength, as well as a different texture to the dish. Keep the dried mushrooms tightly covered and store in a cool, dry place.

Never use canned or frozen mushrooms.

Mancini peppers: This is a brand of canned roasted red peppers that have an excellent taste and texture—they are sweet and succulent. You may, of course, roast your own peppers by charring the skin completely either over a flame or in a very hot oven. Once the skins are blackened, put the peppers in a paper bag, close the bag tightly and let sit for 5 minutes. Remove them from the bag, peel off the skins under cold running water, pull out the stem and remove the seeds.

Potatoes (Patate): I refer to "ricing" potatoes in one of the recipes. This is done with a potato ricer. The cooked, peeled potato passes through the holes in the ricer and comes out in strands.

Tomatoes (Pomodori): Many of the recipes call for peeled and seeded Italian plum tomatoes. I use the cans of imported whole tomatoes that are packed in their own juices. These are already peeled and can be easily seeded by cutting them in half and scooping out the seeds with your finger or passing them through a mesh strainer. Fresh plum tomatoes can also be used when in season. Blanch them briefly to allow you to easily peel the skins. Slice them in half and gently squeeze out the seeds.

Vinegar (Aceto)

There are many types of vinegar, but I use a red wine vinegar more than any other. Buy a full-bodied Italian brand. I also use balsamic vinegar often. This is an Italian vinegar that has been aged for a longer period than a regular vinegar. It is brown in color and has a very special taste. Purchase balsamic vinegar in Italian groceries or specialty food shops. There are many flavored vinegars that you can try in dressings and sauces.

Wine (Vino)

A brief note on cooking wines: Always use a good wine for cooking because it will impart its flavor to the preparations.

A Final Note on Technique:

Reducing a sauce means to cook a sauce, usually over high heat, until it has thickened. As the sauce boils or simmers, the liquid evaporates and the sauce reduces to a thicker state. To "nape" a food with a sauce means to carefully cover it with the sauce.

When sautéing a preparation, use a pan large enough to comfortably hold all the ingredients, i.e., the ingredients should easily have contact with the bottom of the pan and, thus, the heat source. If you do not have a pan large enough, simply use two pans, dividing the ingredients between them.

INDEX